Manage M
for Deeper L

21 evidence-based and easy-to-apply tactics that support memory while learning and beyond

Patti Shank, PhD

Deeper Learning Series

Workplace learning is not known to be research driven but Patti's work is transforming this. In *Manage Memory for Deeper Learning*, Patti translates what is sometimes complex research into actionable tactics that everyone can use. The books in this series are must-read classics on learning design.
Robin Petterd, PhD , Founder, Sprout Labs

This is another must-have book from Patti Shank. Her evidence-based tactics will help you create learning content that is remembered and used. I highly recommend this book.
Guy W. Wallace, President, EPPIC Inc.

Patti has done the heavy lifting and summarized a mountain of learning research that too often is overlooked. The science of learning has never been so easy to understand *and* feasible to apply. This book will help you improve your instruction.
JD Dillon, Chief Learning Architect, Axonify

What I find particularly strong in this book is the clear, concise language, the easy-to-understand examples, and the way Patti helps you to connect the tactics. If you design learning experiences, you simply must understand how your design can make or break what people can remember and why remembering is critical for learning and work.
Mirjam Neelen, Learning Advisory Manager/Learning Experience Design Lead

What does the research say is a waste of time, and maybe even detrimental to learning? Well, if you want to know, Dr. Patti Shank is one of the authors you should be reading. When she writes something, she backs it up with the research support. There are only a precious few authors like this in our training profession. And, you should be reading everything she writes, and praying she writes more. Thank her directly by recommending this book to others. What are you waiting for? Buy this book! I've told you to buy this book.
Bill Sawyer, Director, Global Learning Services, Seal Software

I want my training to be relevant, easily consumable, and effective. I don't want to overwhelm people or waste their time. The tactics in *Manage Memory for Deeper Learning* take the guesswork out and help me make reasoned decisions. The books in this series are easy to read and apply and are a gift to those who want to optimize training experiences.
Karen Hyder, Online Event Producer and Speaker Coach

Patti Shank provides a fascinating explanation of how memory works and how integral it is to learning. She describes four strategies and 21 tactics that help us design instructional programs for deeper learning outcomes. Based on a large body of scientific research, Patti's book is clear, straight-forward, practical, and engaging. I strongly recommend *Manage Memory for Deeper Learning* to instructional designers, trainers, teachers, professors, lecturers, and anyone who wants to help people remember.
Steve Foreman, President, InfoMedia Designs, Inc. and author of *The LMS Guidebook*

Thank *you*

Heidi Matthews and the **ATD Kansas City Chapter** helped me select this topic as the next book in the series. They are likely unaware of the help they provided. I explain their role in the beginning of Chapter 1.

Bill Sawyer, Mirjam Neelen, and Karen Hyder reviewed the book in advance and offered input. These people and others repeatedly make my work better.

The people who recommended the book (cover and inside) read the book before publishing. It's asking for a lot and I'm grateful.

Brent Wilson, Jessica Coon, and the **Auraria Library** at **The University of Colorado, Denver,** make it possible for me to use tools that are expensive and hard to obtain. Without their help, I could not write these books. I am seriously grateful.

Readers are the most important reason for writing. I'm indebted to you.

Table of Contents

Introduction 1
From Memory to Learning 9
    Why Is Memory So Critical? 10
    Dual-channel Processing 19
    Prior Knowledge 20
    Mental Effort (Cognitive Load) 22
    Deep Learning 25
    Learnability/Readability 28
    Four Strategies and 21 Tactics 29
Strategy 1: Understand the Work 31
    Tactic 1: Analyze Prior Knowledge 32
    Tactic 2: Analyze Work Tasks 36
    Tactic 3: Evaluate What Must Be Remembered 40
    Deeper Practice 45
Strategy 2: Eliminate Needless Mental Effort 47
    Tactic 4: Remove Unnecessary Content 48
    Tactic 5: Avoid Split Attention 54
    Tactic 6: Allow Processing Time 65
    Tactic 7: Offer Appropriate Control 68
    Deeper Practice 71
Strategy 3: Make Content Easier to Comprehend 73
    Tactic 8: Use Conventions 74

    Tactic 9: Use *Their* Language 78

    Tactic 10: Add Advance Organizers 82

    Tactic 11: Don't Just Tell: Show.. 86

    Tactic 12: Focus Attention.. 95

    Tactic 13: Chunk Content 99

    Tactic 14: Avoid Multitasking 108

    Tactic 15: Support Memory.. 111

    Deeper Practice.. 117

Strategy 4: Build Deep Understanding (Schemas)................... **119**

    Tactic 16: Supply Missing Knowledge...................................... 120

    Tactic 17: Prefer Direct Instruction.. 125

    Tactic 18: Check and Fix Understanding 129

    Tactic 19: Promote Remembering.. 132

    Tactic 20: Build Worked Examples.. 139

    Tactic 21: Adapt for Prior Knowledge 143

    Deeper Practice.. 145

Now What? **147**

    Retrieval Practice... 149

    Manage Memory for Deeper Learning Checklist 157

    Want More?.. 162

    References 164

Index.. 177

About the Author.. 181

CHAPTER 1

Introduction

It took me a while to settle on a topic for this book. Before I wrote *Write and Organize for Deeper Learning* and *Practice and Feedback for Deeper Learning,* I knew exactly what I wanted to write about. I picked these topics because the tactics improved learning outcomes but were either unknown or ignored.

I've been muddling around over the next book in the Deeper Learning series for months now. Frustrated. And just a few days before writing this book, the next book topic became obvious. You've had that experience, right? Where something that wasn't clear a moment ago is now clear?

I have been writing about memory and tactics for working with the limitations of memory for months. I had just delivered an online session on this topic to the ATD Kansas City chapter. The session started out with technical problems (mine). Audience members had tons of questions and weren't afraid to ask. (I LOVE that!) They wanted to know the whys behind the whats.

The next morning, Heidi Matthews—Training Manager and VP of Programs for ATD Kansas City—let me know that the participants loved the webinar and she had already seen some of them using what we had discussed! (Cue the dance music!) At that moment (okay, the next morning), I realized I had already been working on the next book but hadn't realized it. I would write the book on memory and the tactics that help us work with and not against it. You're holding that book in your hand.

One of the biggest challenges in the workplace is the accelerating rate of change and the need to continually adapt to these changes to survive. These changes have led to major changes in jobs and skills. For example, some jobs—such as parking attendant and accounting clerk—are declining, taken over by technology solutions and applications. And there are jobs that didn't exist 10 years ago, including drone operator and mobile application developer. These jobs came into existence to work with new technologies and systems.

Even more stable jobs no longer have stable skills. For example, weather forecasters now work with complex computer programs and electricians work with technology-driven systems.

These changes are clearly affecting the need to learn in the workplace. In the not-so-distant past, people could learn the skills for their work and the skills stayed relatively stable. But static skills are no longer the norm. Those of us who teach others, then, must help people prepare to update and change job skills as part of growing expertise and remaining employable.

Instruction is a design science. Design sciences such as engineering apply scientific principles to practical human challenges. Fortunately, we have clear and actionable science to tell us how we can help organizations deal with the need for ongoing skill changes. We can look to related sciences, including learning, cognition, attention, training, information design, psychology, and usability to help us design instruction that makes learning easier, more memorable, and more likely to transfer from learning to the job. (Ask me why neuroscience isn't included in that list next time you see me.)

These sciences (and others) tell us how to design for ease of learning, remembering, and application. It starts with understanding human memory. We don't record memories in our mind the way a video recorder records. Building instruction so people will "record" what they see and hear is like buying food and expecting it to "become" dinner. It doesn't work that way.

What we remember and can use as a result of instruction is complicated. It depends more on what we already know about the topic (prior knowledge) than what we see and hear. That's because what we already know gives meaning to what we see and hear. You'll be hearing a lot about prior knowledge in this book, as it's critical to memory and learning.

I said learning is complicated. As an example, I worked in various retail shops when I was a teen and young adult. Retail jobs, like many others, have many facts, steps, and decisions to learn and apply. Even seemingly simple work is complex, once analyzed. In Figure 1.1, I list a few of the facts, concepts, steps, and decisions needed to ring up a sale in this environment as an example. Many of the tasks are interdependent. Complicated.

Figure 1.1 List of facts, concepts, steps, and decision points for ringing up a sale

Facts and Concepts	Steps	Decision Points
Terms: bar code, flash sale, inventory, layaway, loyalty program... *Pricing:* regular, sale, clearance, flash sale...	Steps to ring up a sale: 1. Welcome customer 2. Scan bar code 3. Ask for loyalty card 4. Input loyalty number or explain benefits of joining loyalty program	- No bar code - Price doesn't scan - Price different from tag - Customer doesn't have card or number - Customer has no loyalty card

When you notice the simultaneous elements involved with most job tasks, you can easily understand how learning can use a great deal of mental effort. We cannot show or tell people the process and expect them to remember or do it. They must process it and integrate it with what they already know—then they can use it.

In the rest of this chapter, I will tell you why I started writing these books and offer some ideas on how to use this book to improve training outcomes.

How This Book Works

After this brief introduction, I offer an overview of the science (research) that supports the four strategies and 21 tactics described in the book. I write in mostly non-academic language (but I use some more academic terms when they are useful to know).

I then discuss key research-focused strategies and tactics you should use to make your instruction meet today's learning conditions and organizational needs.

One important note about my use of language. I use the word "knowledge" a lot in this book. In most cases, "knowledge" means both knowledge (knowing about) and skills (knowing how).

Using This Book

This book presents four specific strategies. For each strategy, I discuss actionable tactics you can implement this very moment. Here are the four strategies I will discuss.

Strategy 1: Understand the Work
Strategy 2: Eliminate Needless Mental Effort
Strategy 3: Make Content Easier to Comprehend
Strategy 4: Build Deep Understanding

(You Should) Practice

Throughout this book, I suggest ways to practice the skills listed. But don't wait for me! There are two excellent ways to strengthen your understanding, and I suggest doing both.

- **Summarize** each section in your own words. Research shows that summarizing in your own words helps you understand. Use this instructional method in your courses, too!
- **Apply** each section to your own content. If you know of others who are using this book, share how you apply the tactics. Offer feedback to each other.

When Should You Use These Strategies and Tactics?

This book applies specifically to adult workplace learning. It applies generally to professional development and other applied adult learning settings. If you need people to learn specific skills and use them on the job or elsewhere in life, this book offers specific ways to make your instruction easier to learn and apply.

In the next chapter, "The Science," I begin by discussing the science that supports the strategies and tactics discussed in the rest of the book. Understanding the science helps you understand the choice of strategies and tactics in the rest of the book. For example, why is it so difficult to learn a lot of new information quickly? Why do we need to worry about not overloading people while learning? How can we help people not forget?

I love this content because research shows it makes a real difference in learning outcomes. If you have suggestions for improving it, I want to hear from you. I am self-publishing the Deeper Learning series, so I can easily maintain and update it. You can contact me through the contact form on my website (www.pattishank.com) if you have comments to make it better.

 Try It

To improve *your* learning outcomes from this book, consider using a few self-directed learning tactics before we move on.

- Skim the book's table of contents. What are the *most important* knowledge and skills *you* hope to gain?

- Why are the knowledge and skills you named important to *you*?

- What kinds of practice do you think you will need to gain the knowledge and skills?

CHAPTER 2

From Memory to Learning

Thinking and learning (cognition) researchers have come to critically important conclusions about human memory. One of the most important is that cognition is governed by biological processes just like metabolism and growth. We must understand and work *with* these processes or what we do doesn't work—or causes harm. People and organizations pay the price.

When people are about to have surgery, they refrain from eating many hours before the procedure. Medical personnel are working with digestion processes to prevent serious complications during surgery. Instruction must likewise adapt to the way cognitive processes work.

In this chapter, I discuss attributes and limitations of memory we must understand and use when designing instruction. The how-tos follow this chapter. Memory is key to learning, remembering, and applying. Three memory systems—sensory memory, working memory, and long-term memory—affect how and how well people learn. I discuss those three memory systems first and then I discuss five related areas of science. Figure 2.1 shows the areas of science we'll discuss first and refer to again in the 21 tactics.

Figure 2.1 Science areas that help us design according to how human memory works

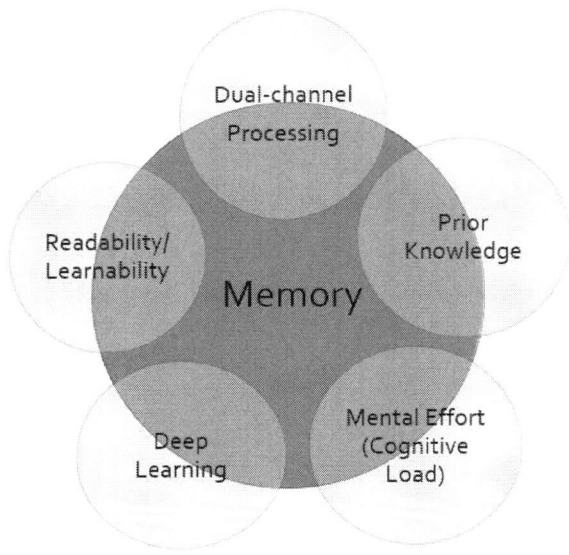

Why Is Memory So Critical?

Decision scientists Saurabh Bhargava, George Loewenstein, and Justin Sydnor completed fascinating research about how people choose healthcare plans. They studied almost 24,000 people in a U.S. Fortune 100 organization that was transitioning to new health care plans.

The entire group of plans had the same coverage but different premiums, deductibles, out-of-pocket maximums, and co-pays. What they found was astounding. A majority chose plans that cost more (in many cases, a lot more) than they needed to. In other words, they could have paid less for the same coverage. This happened not only the first year of implementation, but the following year as well. The researchers figured that workers overspent close to 25% on their coverage.

Analysis showed that the primary cause for overspending was that workers did not have the knowledge to help them find and select a lower-cost plan.

It may not be obvious yet, but the problem in this example is a memory problem. Memory is the *how* behind learning, thinking, and problem solving. Memory is used to *process* what we are learning, *store* what we know, and *use* what we know. Most workers didn't have the knowledge they needed to make this decision.

This healthcare plan choice example showcases the tangible and very real cost of not having needed knowledge. I wrote *Managing Memory for Deeper Learning* so you will know how to work *with* the biological processes for thinking and memory that help people learn, remember, and apply. We'll next discuss the attributes and limitations of the three memory systems.

Sensory Memory

Processing new information starts with what our senses bring into awareness (Figure 2.2). The environment produces a lot of sensory information (such as what we see and hear around us).

Figure 2.2 Sensory memory

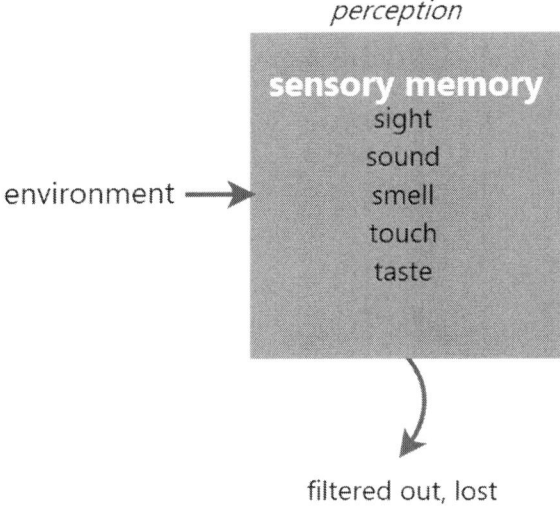

Sensory memories are fleeting... less than a second. Want to experience sensory memory for yourself? Stare at Figure 2.2 and then shut your eyes. Try this a few times (stare at Figure 2.2 and then shut your eyes). When you close your eyes, you are likely to "see" Figure 2.2 in your mind for an instant.

Sensory information that isn't brought to awareness is lost. Typically, our mind decides what's meaningful and worth being aware of based on what we already know (prior knowledge) and inborn reactions (loud noises, anything that could be a threat).

Working Memory

When we perceive sensory information as meaningful, working memory starts processing it (Figure 2.3). A large part of processing includes making sense of the information. We understand what we are processing based on prior knowledge.

Figure 2.3 Sensory memory and working memory

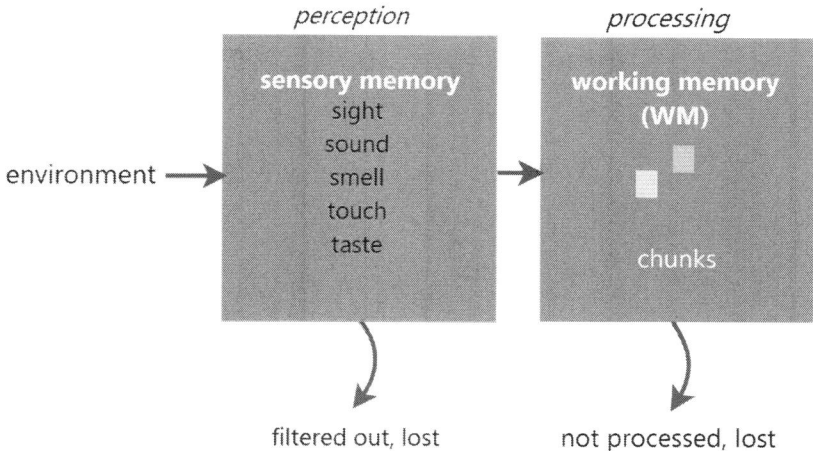

We use working memory to think, reason, and learn. But working memory is limited in how much it can process (only a few chunks of information at a time) and how long it can hold it.

If you are at a store and want to know if you have enough cash on hand to make a purchase of $0.25 and $6.60, you can typically add these numbers in your head. There isn't a lot to remember as you "process" the addition. But, if you are at the grocery store later that day trying to decide if you have enough in your checking account to cover the 14 items in your cart, you likely won't do this in your head because there is too much to process simultaneously. You need help: paper, cell phone calculator, etc.

Long-term Memory

We decide which environmental information to perceive based largely on prior knowledge. We make meaning from what we are processing in working memory based on prior knowledge. Well, *where is* this prior knowledge we are using? Prior knowledge is what we already know—stored in organized knowledge structures called *schemas* (Figure 2.4).

Figure 2.4 Sensory memory, working memory, and long-term memory

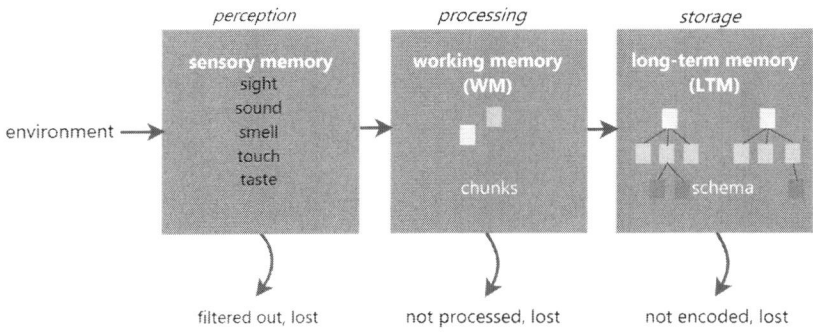

Long-term memory stores information with related information in schemas. We can remember the word *schema* more easily by understanding that *schema* and *schematic* come from the same root. A schematic is a drawing or diagram that shows the main parts and relationships of the parts. Schemas organize what we know. Both come from the root word *scheme*, meaning a group of related things or parts.

Information stored in schemas helps us makes sense of information we are processing—and schemas are used to perform. Schemas can be simple or complex, depending on how much we know. A beginning schema for how to maintain a car, for example, may include only that a car needs maintenance every so often. More complex schemas for car maintenance may include types of maintenance for different car systems and when we need to perform them.

Learning changes schemas. Although (we think) long-term memory can hold an unlimited amount of information, stored information may be more or less easy to recall. It is harder to recall rarely-used information, for instance, than information we recall often. In workplace learning, we must help people develop schemas and make information in schemas easier to recall and use. Two primary goals when designing instructional content include:
1. Manage processing in working memory
2. Build accurate and usable schemas in long-term memory

Encoding into long-term memory and retrieval from long-term memory show that we use LTM and WM together when thinking and learning. Figure 2.5 shows these processes.

Figure 2.5 Encoding into LTM and retrieval from LTM

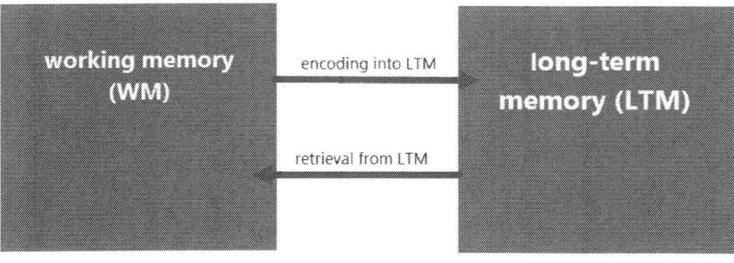

Encoding

After processing new information in working memory, we must store that information if we want to remember or use it. We call this process *encoding*. We can remember the word *encoding* as memory **codes** in our mind. There are three main ways we believe we encode information:

- Visually, as images
- Auditorily, as sounds
- Semantically, as meaning

Most encoding is semantic. Encoding semantically means we store information along with the context (situation, emotions, location, etc.). Therefore, one strategy we use to help people remember what they learn in training is to teach using the same context as the job.

For better encoding, instruction must include activities that help people process the information deeply, in a way that allows for easier retrieval. Encoding isn't an event but a process. It can begin during training, but people can easily forget what they don't regularly use. So, we must also provide practice for remembering after training.

Retrieval

Remembering means retrieving information from long-term memory (LTM). We more easily retrieve what we find meaningful. Therefore, it' critical that we make instruction personally meaningful and relevant to a person's work or life. Research says that, for long-term retrieval, people should learn the same way they will use the information.

For example, if people find needed information using a specific tool on the job, they find information using that tool during training.

The following are a few of the most important implications of memory for instruction.
- ✓ WM is a limited resource. We must take its constraints into account when creating information and instruction.
- ✓ We need to design with as few unnecessary demands on WM as possible, so people can deal with the demands of learning.
- ✓ We want people to deeply process what they are learning during training.

 **Try It**

To improve your understanding and make it easier to remember, describe what you think is most important to remember about sensory memory, working memory, long-term memory, encoding, and retrieval.

sensory memory

working memory

long-term memory

encoding

retrieval

In the rest of this chapter, I'll discuss five areas of research—dual-channel processing, prior knowledge, cognitive load, deep learning, and readability/learnability—that help us understanding how to work with the attributes and limitations of memory.

Dual-channel Processing

Dual-channel processing refers to separate visual (anything initially processed by the eyes, such as images and text) and verbal (anything processed by the ears, such as speech) processing sub-systems in working memory. We also have visual and verbal sub-systems to store information in long-term memory. Using both channels simultaneously can share the processing load.

One of the most common examples of dual processing to help learning is using narration to explain images rather than text. When we combine still or moving visuals with narration we are using both channels. When everything we present is visual (images, video, text), the visual channel may get overloaded. Using both channels can also improve remembering because people are able to store information in two ways.

> The following are some important implications of dual-channel processing for instruction.
> - ✓ Rather than use text that must be processed with images, use narration to reduce the load on the visual processing sub-system.
> - ✓ Don't overload total working memory, so dual-channel processing can be effective.

Using both channels can reduce the processing load and improve the ability to retrieve.

 **Try It**

To improve your understanding and make it easier to remember, describe what you think is most important to remember about dual-channel processing and why it is critical to learning on the job.

Prior Knowledge

Prior knowledge is organized information stored in long-term memory as schemas. It's our long-term memory's storage of what we know. Prior knowledge is not static as, when we learn, it changes what we know.

Knowing how much and what types of prior knowledge our audience has helps us make instruction relevant to their needs, and help people construct accurate and usable schemas.

If people have *inadequate* or *incorrect* prior knowledge, it is difficult to accurately learn and understand.

The more complete, accurate, and usable our schemas are, the easier it is to use them in work situations. Figure 2.6 shows different components of prior knowledge and how increasingly deep knowledge contributes to application.

Prior knowledge components toward the left side of Figure 2.6 are a necessary foundation but not enough for application. As we are able to add knowledge components towards the right side of Figure 2.6, application is more possible.

Figure 2.6 Components of prior knowledge with examples (adapted from Hailikari, T., Katajavuori, N., & Lindblom-Ylanne, S., 2008).

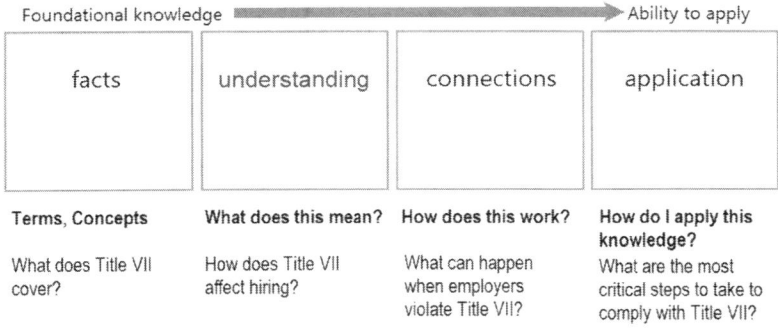

Because prior knowledge helps us understand new information, people with more prior knowledge find it easier to learn more information. An experienced optician knows how different eyeglass lens materials work for different prescriptions. When new lens materials are available, she can add the new lens material specifications to her lens material schema and apply this knowledge when filling glasses prescriptions.

When we know very little, we must try to process new information in a vacuum—making less informed decisions. When people have no schema, they won't say, "Can you help me build complete, accurate, and usable schemas?" What they say instead is that they don't understand or are confused or don't know how to proceed. Or they say nothing.

Building schemas is one of the most important outcomes of deep learning. Accurate and usable schemas help us do our work, solve problems, and continue to learn.

Prior knowledge (schema) reduces the load on working memory because what we know helps us process and organize new information.

> The following are some of the most important implications of prior knowledge for instruction. We:
> - ✓ Need to connect what we are teaching to what people already know. This helps information stick.
> - ✓ Cannot assume people understand the information we present. We need to figure out if they do.

Try It

To improve your understanding and make it easier to remember, describe what you think is most important to remember about how prior knowledge supports learning.

Mental Effort (Cognitive Load)

Since learning requires conscious and unconscious effort, we should carefully channel the effort in ways that help and do not harm learning. We call the amount of mental effort used by working memory *cognitive load*. This understanding began with the work of John Sweller, an influential Australian educational psychologist and researcher. He helped us understand what causes cognitive load and what we can do to reduce or manage it.

Researchers discuss different types of cognitive load. To make these complex discussions more concise, I'm referring to two categories of cognitive load: damaging and needed (Figure 2.7). Damaging cognitive load is caused by problematic design. It uses up mental effort without helping people learn, remember, or apply. Needed cognitive load is the effort needed to learn.

Figure 2.7 Damaging cognitive load (top) and needed cognitive load (bottom)

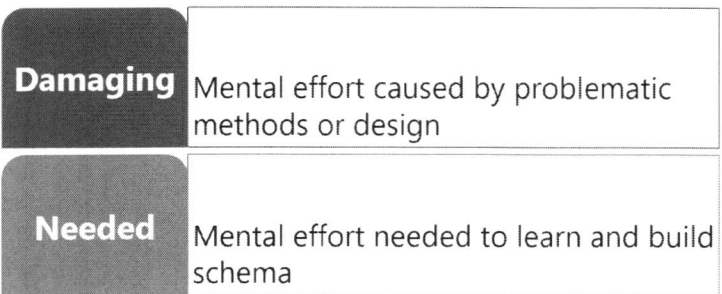

Damaging cognitive load wastes mental effort better used for needed cognitive load. Since working memory has limitations, we must reduce or eliminate damaging cognitive load. The following are examples of problems that cause damaging cognitive load:
- Content that is not essential for the learning objectives
- Non-valuable or decorative graphics
- Unnecessary or redundant explanations
- Images (still [like pictures] and moving [like animations

or video]) that are in a different place or time from their explanation
- Media that doesn't offer stopping, starting, and rewinding

Needed cognitive load helps us learn, but it needs to be managed so people do not have too much at a time. The following are examples of needed cognitive load:
- Learning simpler and foundational content before learning more complex content
- Activities that deepen understanding
- Varied practices that improve application

We must reduce or eliminate damaging cognitive load and manage helpful cognitive load.

> The following are some of the most important implications of cognitive load for instruction.
> ✓ Eliminate as much damaging cognitive load as possible.
> ✓ Manage needed cognitive load so there isn't too much at a time.

 **Try It**

To improve your understanding and make it easier to remember, describe what you think is most important to remember about how cognitive load affects learning.

Deep Learning

In the 1970s, "depth" of learning became "a thing." Two professors at the University of Gothenburg—Ference Marton and Roger Säljö—did groundbreaking research on depth of processing while learning, which began a conversation about (and research into) what they called *surface* and *deep learning approaches.*

A surface approach focuses on facts and points. A deep approach searches for meaning, relationships, and integration with prior knowledge.

Robert Bjork, Professor of Psychology at the University of California—and a well-known researcher and writer on memory and learning—has written extensively on the topic of "desirable difficulties." Bjork's research shows that deep processing is critical to being able to apply what we learn. These desirable difficulties are important for deep learning.

Table 2.1 shows primary differences between surface and deeper learning approaches. A shallower approach—for example, what terms and concepts mean—is often the first step to deeper learning. But this is not enough for application (we previously discussed how certain prior knowledge components are necessary but insufficient to help people apply).

Table 2.1 Differences between surface and deep learning approaches

	Reason for Learning	*Learning Tasks*
Surface	Short-term use, for course requirements or testing	- Enough effort to meet requirements - Accept concepts at face value - Remember content, if needed
Deep	Long-term use, for application	- Effortful understanding - Relate content to already-known information - Find underlying patterns and principles - Apply learning to personally important problems - Critically examine logic - Come to conclusions

Opticians in training learn physics concepts and terminology, such as refraction and diopters, without knowing how to use them. Without going further, those concepts don't have much context, and this makes it hard to remember them—and difficult to use them. As they learn to work with real prescriptions, these concepts are applied to specific work tasks such as selecting lens materials for a specific prescription.

> The following are some of the most important implications of deep learning for instruction.
> ✓ We should help people learn deeply—both in formal instruction and on their own—as jobs are becoming less routine and more complex.
> ✓ Deep learning supports usable skills.

Try It

To improve your understanding and make it easier to remember, describe what you think is most important to remember about how deep learning is different from surface learning.

Learnability/Readability

Learnability is the ease and speed with which something can be learned, remembered, and applied. Learnability applied to learning in organizations means people can easily use instruction, performance support, and other content to get work done and improve skills (complete tasks, fix problems, and so on).

In *Write and Organize for Deeper Learning,* I discussed how readability impacts ability to understand and use. Readability is the ease with which people can read and understand text. We can compute readability statistics as a first step in writing for our audience's needs.

> The following are two of the most important implications of learnability for instruction.
> - ✓ Learnability means designing for good readability and ease of use.
> - ✓ Making information and instruction readable and usable reduces cognitive load and makes it easier to learn.

 Try It

To improve your understanding and make it easier to remember, describe what you think is most important to remember about how learnability affects learning.

Four Strategies and 21 Tactics

Table 2.2 lists the four strategies and 21 tactics discussed in the next five chapters. Consider bookmarking this page as it offers an at-a-glance view of all the strategies and tactics that work together for managing memory during instruction.

Table 2.2 Managing memory strategies and tactics

Chapter 3	**Strategy 1: Understand the Work**	Tactic 1: Analyze Prior Knowledge Tactic 2: Analyze Work Tasks Tactic 3: Evaluate What Must Be Remembered
Chapter 4	**Strategy 2: Eliminate Needless Mental Effort**	Tactic 4: Remove Unnecessary Content Tactic 5: Avoid Split Attention Tactic 6: Allow Processing Time Tactic 7: Offer Appropriate Control
Chapter 5	**Strategy 3: Make Content Easier to Comprehend**	Tactic 8: Use Conventions Tactic 9: Use *Their* Language Tactic 10: Add Advance Organizers Tactic 11: Don't Just Tell: Show Tactic 12: Focus Attention Tactic 13: Chunk Content Tactic 14: Avoid Multitasking Tactic 15: Support Memory
Chapter 6	**Strategy 4: Build Deep Understanding (Schemas)**	Tactic 16: Supply Missing Knowledge Tactic 17: Prefer Direct Instruction Tactic 18: Check and Fix Understanding Tactic 19: Promote Remembering Tactic 20: Build Worked Examples Tactic 21: Adapt for Prior Knowledge

CHAPTER 3

Strategy 1: Understand the Work

We must understand the work people do to help them do their work and learn new skills. For example, when Maria is checking in patients at the front desk of a dental office, we can observe the steps used to check patients in.

1. Check in patient.
2. Verify insurance information.
3. Request copay, if applicable.
4. Offer an estimated waiting time.

But we don't "see" the decisions she is making during each step. When she verifies insurance information, changes to this information may trigger added steps. After she verifies or changes insurance information, she may need to confirm insurance coverage and find out what benefits the patient has. These are just simple examples of how decision points impact tasks.

If we needed to train the people at the front desk about new medical privacy laws, for example, we would need to understand how these changes ripple through their tasks and sub-tasks.

Without doing the analysis steps discussed in this chapter, we won't be able to design job- and task-focused training and won't have adequate information to select the best memory tactics for the situation.

Knowing what people need to be able to DO is a critical first step toward designing for deep learning.

We discuss these analysis steps in Tactics 1-3 (Figure 3.1).

Figure 3.1 Tactics that help us understand the work
> **Tactic 1: Analyze Prior Knowledge**
> **Tactic 2: Analyze Work Tasks**
> **Tactic 3: Evaluate What Must Be Remembered**

Tactic 1: Analyze Prior Knowledge

Because prior knowledge is so important to learning, we need to identify the prior knowledge of our audience so we know what people need to learn. Many tactics in this book have different recommendations depending on the audience's level of prior knowledge.

It's not easy to know how much prior knowledge people have. We commonly count on indirect measures of knowledge, which are an imperfect way to know what the audience already knows. Table 3.1 shows common indirect methods for finding out what people already know.

Asking workers or their supervisors to estimate what they know is imprecise. People with less knowledge tend to think they know more and people with more knowledge tend to think they know less.

Table 3.1 Indirect measures of prior knowledge

Indirect measures of prior knowledge (perceived knowledge)

Self-report	Ask people to estimate their own knowledge.
Supervisor reports	Have supervisors judge the knowledge their direct reports have.
Previous courses	Review courses and self-directed learning.
Job description/ tenure	Use the job description and length of time in a specific job.

Direct measures of knowledge and skill—such as measuring actual job tasks and outcomes—are more accurate, but this process takes time. Taking fewer measurements may be inadequate, as performance can change based on personal and work factors.

Slava Kalyuga (Professor, School of Education at the University of New South Wales) and John Sweller (Emeritus Professor, School of Education, at the University of New South Wales—we discussed his work in the last chapter) are prolific researchers in cognitive load. They offer a simple but valid way to assess prior knowledge in a specific area.

Because people with more prior knowledge have more complete and accurate schema, we can *infer* prior knowledge by asking people to solve a problem that depends on that knowledge. They suggest using more intermediate-level knowledge, as this type of knowledge is better for distinguishing between more and less prior knowledge.

To assess prior knowledge of a system, for example, we can ask people to give us the next step for a problem (Figure 3.2).

Figure 3.2 Task calling for intermediate-level knowledge

The following dialog box appears after adding two procedure codes for Nancy Smith.

```
┌─────────────────────────────────────┐
│                                   x │
│   Wrong location.                   │
│                                     │
│                                     │
└─────────────────────────────────────┘
```

What is the next step?

Figure 3.2 asks people to recall intermediate-level knowledge. Asking people for the next step in the login process, on the other hand, would be beginner-level knowledge.

Ideal analysis uses various sources of data. We may use a combination of indirect and direct measures for this purpose. For example, for the system training, we may start by asking people to check off topics and sub-topics they already know and feel they don't need additional training on. We can get information about common mistakes. And we can use Kalyuga's and Sweller's process of asking people for the next step. This type of information gives us a picture of what people do and do not need.

People get nervous about "collecting and analyzing data" because it seems mysterious and hard. But the ideas in this tactic are simple and don't require statistical or qualitative data analysis. We apply these ideas by

1. Selecting sources of information.
2. Collecting information.
3. Reviewing the information to see what people know and don't know.

4. Using the information to choose tactics that work best for the level of prior knowledge.

We combine analyzing prior knowledge with analyzing work to know what people need to know (Tactic 2), and how much they already know (this tactic).

Figure 3.3 shows an example of direct and indirect measures to analyze specific hazardous materials knowledge.

Figure 3.3 Direct (left) and indirect (right) analysis for DECIDE skills

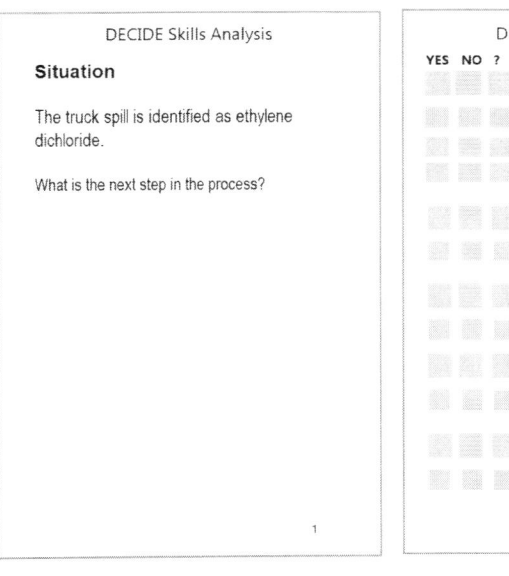

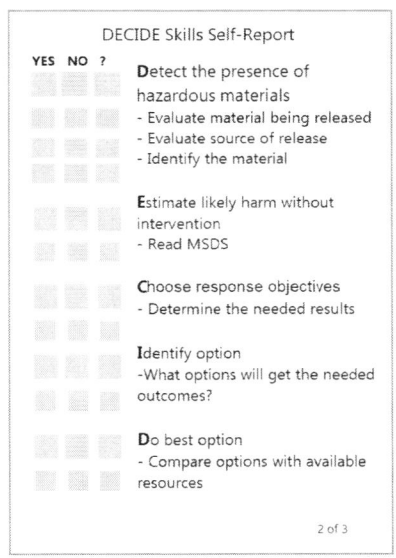

DECIDE Skills Analysis

Situation

The truck spill is identified as ethylene dichloride.

What is the next step in the process?

DECIDE Skills Self-Report

YES NO ?

Detect the presence of hazardous materials
- Evaluate material being released
- Evaluate source of release
- Identify the material

Estimate likely harm without intervention
- Read MSDS

Choose response objectives
- Determine the needed results

Identify option
-What options will get the needed outcomes?

Do best option
- Compare options with available resources

Tactic 2: Analyze Work Tasks

Understanding work tasks helps us build instruction that meets job-specific needs. Here are some of the more common work task analysis processes.

1. Document how people complete work tasks, including
   1.1. The tasks and sub-tasks completed
   1.2. Knowledge needed to perform these tasks and sub-tasks
   1.3. Tools and materials used
   1.4. Decisions made while performing
   1.5. Common problems, how to troubleshoot
   1.6. Outcomes of work tasks and sub-tasks
2. Create task-focused instructional objectives
3. Select strategies and tactics appropriate for meeting the objectives
4. Sequence and chunk instruction for the audience and tasks

I'm a realist and understand that the average person who designs instruction won't do all of these (but your instruction would be stronger and have better outcomes if you did). If you're reading this book, however, I believe you're willing to do more to get optimal results, so I'll share a minimalist version.

Performing a minimalist work task analysis tells us what people do, how they do it, and problems that get in the way. It helps us understand the memory demands of work tasks. Table 3.2 shows a concise analysis of the first two steps and decision points for checking a patient in at a medical office.

Table 3.2 Documentation of steps, sub-steps, typical problems, and decision points

Steps and Sub-steps	Problems	Decision Points
Check in patient - Greet patient - Check into system - Make changes	Appointment not in system Patient not in system	Reschedule? Fit in? Add patient? Wrong information?
Obtain insurance information - Get and update info - Verify coverage	Insurance doesn't cover the visit/procedure	Problems with insurance? Impact of insurance on visit?

Most people think it's best to work with content experts to gain this information. But experts (with extensive and long-held prior knowledge) typically don't do tasks the way other people do. They may add, skip, or combine steps, and so forth. Because of their expertise, they often don't understand what people with less knowledge do. What experts tell you may be *their* process alone—and not a process that people with lesser knowledge can follow.

Experts' deep knowledge allows them to perform without having to think through the steps. This is one of the benefits of accurate and usable schemas, but it creates a challenge for getting detailed information about tasks and sub-tasks from them. So, it's better to observe and talk to people who have consistent and excellent outcomes, but who remember the sub-steps, issues, problems, and decisions.

If the task is new and there are no excellent performers yet, you can ask content experts to offer what is thought to be the best process. Getting the steps and sub-steps from a content expert has the problems I mentioned, however. If you are working with content expert data, you should revisit the task once people start to do it to find out what works and what doesn't. This will help you pinpoint the right steps and sub-steps, problems, and decision points.

Some people tell me they can't analyze tasks. Someone hands them content and they use it to build a course. My response: That's like building a house without blueprints. Really. Bad. Idea.

Do you see your job as merely building content? Or are you building instructional content—including what is needed to help people learn, maintain, or advance work-related skills?

Understanding the work is necessary for designing job- and task-oriented instruction.

⮕ Resource

What we discussed in this tactic is a limited form of task analysis. I simplified it a great deal and this approach will likely get you helpful information. If you want to learn more, I recommend Guy Wallace's chapter in the *Handbook of Human Performance Technology, Third Edition*. Guy has very deep skills in understanding work and that's why I asked him if I could include this resource.

In this chapter, he describes the need to model mastery performance and how to systematically figure out what needs to be in place to create and support it. It's very valuable work. His chapter is available here: https://eppicinc.files.wordpress.com/2012/01/chapter-11-wallace-handbook-of-hpt_third-edition-2006.pdf.

Also review materials on Guy's website at https://eppic.biz. And consider the book *Working Minds: A Practitioner's Guide to Cognitive Task Analysis,* written by Beth Crandall, Gary A. Klein and Robert R. Hoffman.

Tactic 3: Evaluate What Must Be Remembered

One reason we *must* understand job tasks is to understand what information and skills people must remember to do their job. We can use tactics for helping people remember, but we first must understand what needs to be remembered!

Table 3.3 shows the previous analysis of the first two steps for checking a patient in at a medical office and obtaining insurance information. I added a fourth column, which shows the knowledge needed to perform the step and sub-steps, handle problems, and correctly make decisions. Some steps, sub-steps, and decisions require people to remember what to do (R) and what to look up (LU).

Table 3.3 Steps, sub-steps, typical problems, decision points, and needed knowledge

Steps and Sub-steps	Problems	Decision Points	Knowledge Needed
Check in patient - Greet patient - Check into system - Make changes	Appointment not in system Patient not in system	Reschedule? Fit in? Add patient? Wrong information?	Adequate greeting (R) Check-in procedure (R) Find another appointment (R)
Obtain insurance information - Get and update info - Verify coverage	Insurance doesn't cover the visit/procedure	Problems with insurance? Impact of insurance on visit?	Insurance check-in (R, LU) Coverage and limits (LU)

I've heard nonsense about how technology makes it possible to no longer need to remember anything to do your job. Ridiculous! Here are four reasons why that makes no sense.
1. Without prior knowledge, we often don't know what to look up.
2. Prior knowledge is needed to interpret what we find when we look things up.
3. Things you look up may be inaccurate, biased, or out of date. Prior knowledge helps you analyze these factors.
4. Work efficiency would plummet if everything had to be looked up.

If you don't understand what I mean, watch this video on YouTube and you'll understand why we cannot have people look everything up. Plus, it's funny!
https://www.youtube.com/watch?v=nF_C3bO8WZ0

Accurate and usable prior knowledge is the engine that drives easier learning and performance.

What if you are having problems connecting to the Internet, for example, and the help desk tells you to open the command prompt and use ping to verify network connectivity? For many non-technical people, this sounds like Klingon (ping. qej ping nuq?). I'm sure you can think of many times where you didn't know what to look up because you didn't have adequate knowledge—or what you looked up didn't make sense to you.

We *can* look up how to do some things when we need help—especially when there is time to do so *and* we have prior knowledge. For example, a friend bought a house and the toilets didn't work well. He read about the best toilets online and then bought them at a large hardware store along with the tools and items he needed. Online job aids and videos showed the replacement steps. But, someone who didn't have needed prior knowledge (what the terminology means, how to use the tools, etc.) would need that knowledge to understand the steps and processes.

Figure 3.4 shows a remembering continuum that helps us consider how well people need to be able to remember what they are learning.

Figure 3.4 Remembering continuum

Look up ← Remember → Automate

"Remember" and "automate" may sound like the same thing, but they're different. "Remember" means being able to recall and use prior knowledge. "Automate" means remembering and using *without effort*. People almost always need automated skills in life-and-death situations—for example, CPR and advanced life-support skills. There are other skills police, military, medical, and emergency personnel have that must be automated. People who do that work regularly practice maintaining automated skills.

Skills used regularly may become almost or completely automated from use. Skills not used regularly typically decline. Knowing whether we should train for remembering—and, if remembered, how easily remembered—is part of the job of designing deep instruction. We'll discuss automating remembering in more detail in Tactic 19.

Table 3.4 offers questions that help analyze the need for

remembering during *and* after training.

Table 3.4 Questions that help analyze the need for remembering

1. Can they look it up on the job?	• Do they have time to look it up? • Do they know how and what to look up? • Will they understand what they look up? • Does the information change regularly?
2. Do they *need* to remember?	• Do they have to perform quickly and with accuracy? • Are they expected to know? • Do they need to remember to perform other job tasks?

Answering *yes* to all the number 1 questions likely means people *do not* need to commit the information or skill to memory. For example, answering customers' questions about the availability of an item likely falls into the can-look-it-up category. The service rep is unlikely to remember the availability of every product and typically uses an application to check stock. They have the prior knowledge to know how to look up stock information and will understand the information they find. That's the job.

The last bullet point in 1 (changing information) points to a *need* to look up the information, as the information changes regularly. Item availability may fall into this category.

Answering *yes* to all or most of the number 2 questions likely means people must commit the knowledge to memory. For example, we expect the emergency veterinarian to act quickly and with accuracy when treating a hurt animal. We expect them to know what questions to ask about the injury and what to do with that information.

If I haven't completely convinced you that remembering is part of needed performance, consider this situation. When you call for technical support and every question you ask requires putting you on hold (to look information up), how confident are you of the knowledge level of the person you are working with? Exactly.

Deeper Practice

We have reached the end of the tactics for **Strategy 1: Understand the Work.** Select the instruction you want—or someone has asked you—to build. Then use the tactics in this chapter (recapped below) to analyze the job context for this training.

Tactic 1	Analyze Prior Knowledge Figure out which direct and indirect methods you can use to find out the prior knowledge level of your audience.
Tactic 2	Analyze Work Tasks Document the tasks and sub-tasks, problems, decisions, and knowledge elements for tasks to be learned.
Tactic 3	Evaluate What Must Be Remembered Find out what people need to commit to memory and what they can look up. Where on the remembering continuum is what they need to remember?

Consider doing this exercise with a group of people so you can discuss the following with others:
- What was helpful, less helpful?
- What did you learn?
- Which parts of this exercise will you continue to use in the future?

CHAPTER 4

Strategy 2: Eliminate Needless Mental Effort

Designing for memory requires removing *unnecessary* demands on working memory. Doing this frees limited working memory for processing information and building schemas. The following typical-but-unfortunate issues cause needless mental effort and decrease the amount of mental effort available to learn.

- Unnecessary content (Tactic 4)
- Content that causes split attention (Tactic 5)
- Content that moves fast and doesn't allow for needed processing (Tactic 6)
- Inappropriate control of the learning environment (Tactic 7)

We describe the nature of these problems and solutions in Tactics 4-7 (Figure 4.1). Although I often show examples of eLearning and technology-based instruction, the tactics (here and in other chapters) apply equally to classroom and blended learning.

Figure 4.1 Tactics that reduce needless mental effort

Tactic 4: Remove Unnecessary Content
Tactic 5: Avoid Split Attention
Tactic 6: Allow Processing Time
Tactic 7: Offer Appropriate Control

Tactic 4: Remove Unnecessary Content

Removing unnecessary demands on working memory while learning frees working memory to process information and build schemas. Below are common content problems that cause harmful cognitive load and interfere with learning during instruction.

- Decorative pictures
- Background music
- Bells and whistles
- "Extra" content

Decorative pictures are pictures that do not offer valuable information—but use memory resources nonetheless. Figure 4.2 shows an example of a decorative picture on a content page. This picture doesn't offer valuable information but uses mental effort.

Figure 4.2 Decorative picture example

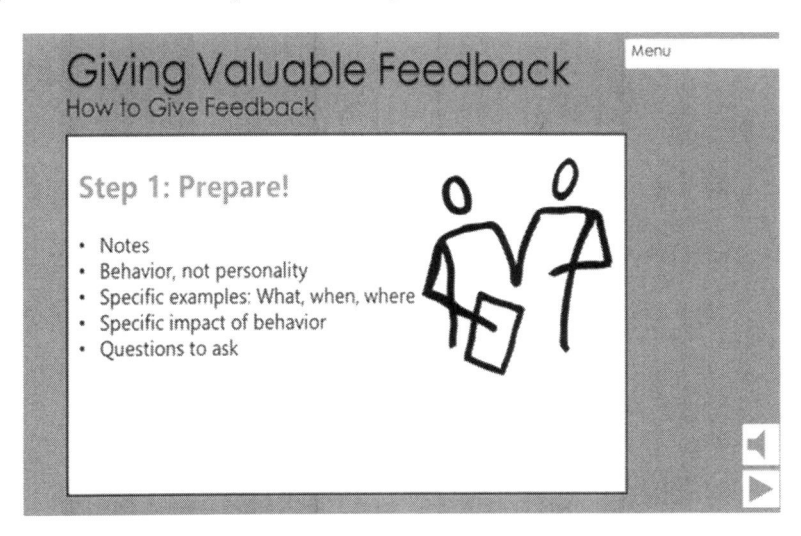

Decorative pictures and background music distract focus away from critical content. Bells and whistles (sound effects, moving text, dancing pigs, etc.) also divert attention from what is important. Unnecessary content distracts attention and focus and makes these critical learning tasks harder.
- Making sense of new information
- Processing content
- Recognizing what is important
- Building schemas

Extra content added "just in case" uses extra effort to process—or, at least, to figure out if it is useful or needed. People using instruction should not suffer because we didn't tie instruction to specific job needs. Figure 4.3 shows a screen from a ladder safety course for construction workers with non-valuable content. What content do you see that shouldn't be there?

Figure 4.3 Non-valuable content example (public domain image from Wikimedia: https://commons.wikimedia.org/wiki/File%3ANow_Where_Did_I_Leave_That_Hammer%3F_(recto)_Your_First_Accident_(verso)_Art.IWMPST14482.jpg)

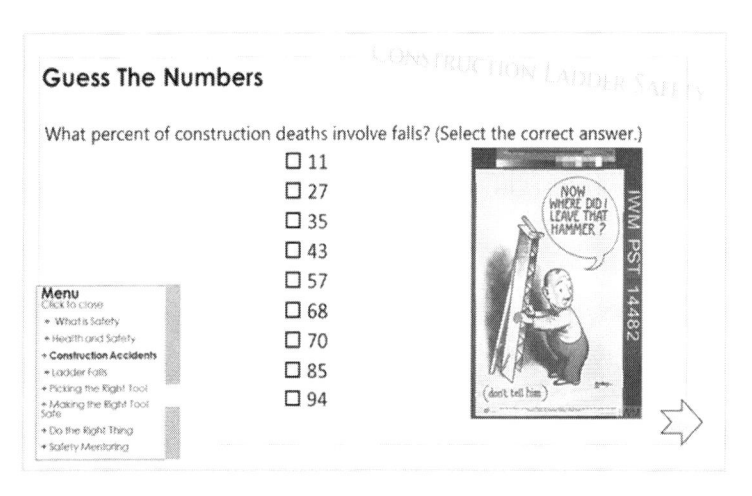

My opinion about the page shown in Figure 4.3 is that most of the content is off-target. The course isn't about general construction accidents. It's about preventing accidents *with ladders*—so the content on the slide does not apply to the learning objectives. Should people have to remember the *exact* percentage of construction accidents that result in death? Putting in a silly cartoon takes attention away a serious issue and sends the wrong message.

Try It

Review the high-level storyboard in Table 4.1 for an employment discrimination lesson for new supervisors. Which elements do you think are unnecessary? My answer is on the next page, but you will learn far more by answering before reading mine!

Table 4.1 High-level lesson storyboard

Lesson: Employment Discrimination/Title I

Topic	Activities	Media
What is employment discrimination/Title I		Audio: Employee describing her case
Types of employment discrimination	Match case to discrimination type	Pictures of angry employees Images of court documents
Legal consequences and remedies of employment discrimination	Select the court cases that resulted in a finding of employment discrimination.	Pictures of people in the courtroom Images of court documents
Employment discrimination policies	Scenarios: What policy applies Application exercises	Typical policies Video: Applying the policy
Resources: Title I Links to relevant cases		

Patti's Response

The items in callouts are likely unnecessary.

Table 4.1 High-level lesson storyboard

Lesson: Employment Discrimination/Title I

Topic	Activities	Media
What is employment discrimination/Title I		Audio: Employee describing her case
Types of employment discrimination	Match case to discrimination [Two unnecessary decorative pictures]	Pictures of angry employees / Images of court documents
Legal consequences and remedies of employment discrimination	[Two unnecessary decorative pictures]	Pictures of people in the courtroom / Images of court documents
Employment discrimination policies	[The lesson didn't cover Title I. The cases make sense for lawyers but that isn't the audience.]	Typical policies / Video: Applying the policy
Resources: Title I Links to of relevant cases		

Bonus question! What information do participants need to *remember* (R) and what can they *look up* (LU)?

	R	LU
Definition of employment discrimination		
What creates employment discrimination		
Company policies		
Steps to follow to apply the policies		

Patti's Response

	R	LU
Definition of employment discrimination	√	
What creates employment discrimination	√	
Company policies	√	√
Steps to follow to apply the policies		√

The first two items are basic knowledge that help participants know how and when they should act and how to find the information they need. The last two items tell what to do in specific situations.

When I wrote this exercise, I put "Company policies" in the LU column. Mirjam Neelen—who reviewed the book prior to publication and offered much-needed insights—said, "Company policies is debatable. Policies describe how you are expected to respond to situations. You need to remember at least at a high level how they apply to your work." She is right, so I changed it to *both* R and LU. (Thank you, Mirjam.)

Since we left out the analysis, context may change what people must remember and what they can look up. For example, a lawyer arguing an employment discrimination case in front of a judge may need to remember far more than a supervisor.

Tactic 5: Avoid Split Attention

Split attention requires people to hold one source of information in memory to understand another source of information. Here's an example from everyday life: reading and remembering instructions for putting the shelves in your new refrigerator and then putting the shelves in. You may go back and forth between the instructions and putting the shelves in as it's hard to remember all the details.

Split attention makes people split their attention between information sources, hold some pieces in memory, and mentally integrate them to understand them. Here's a common example in instructional content: the need to split attention between content elements (such as a diagram and a text explanation) to understand them. Or splitting attention between content elements shown at different times (for example, background information for an activity on one screen and the directions for the activity on another screen).

Split attention occurs regularly in print materials when text explanations and images (such as diagram and charts) require readers to mentally integrate information in the text with information in the diagram or chart. I show an example in Figure 4.4.

Figure 4.4 Split attention example with image and text

Name: Jane Olsson			Date: 10/17/2017		
	Spherical	Cylinder	Axis	Add	Prism
OD	-4.75	+2.25	090	+2.00	
OS	-4.00	+2.25	090	+2.25	

Marcus Phillips   O.D.   License: 149861

- **OD**: Right
- **OS**: Left
- **Sphere**: Lens power to correct myopia
- **Cylinder**: Lens power needed to correct astigmatism
- **Axis**: The orientation of astigmatism in degrees
- **Prism**: Lens power to compensate for alignment problems.
- **Add**: Added lens power for reading.

In many print and digital materials, for space and formatting reasons, images end up where they fit—not *with* the explanation. This makes readers go back and forth between the image and related text.

Digital materials often ask people to integrate content from various sources, including links, text, audio, and still and moving images. These content items may not be physically in the same location. Although research shows that a mix of text, audio, and still or moving images *can* help people understand, they can also cause problems for understanding when we disconnect materials in time or place.

Table 4.2 shows common instructional situations that cause split attention—and what research tells us is the fix.

Table 4.2 Common situations that require split attention

Situation	Problem	Fix
Image, video, diagram, or animation + explanatory text	Need to hold explanatory text in working memory to interpret the image, video, or animation.	Integrate the image, video, or animation with a concise version of explanatory text. Use concise audio to explain the image, video, diagram, or animation to use both visual and verbal processing.
Example + explanatory text	Need to hold explanatory text in working memory to interpret the example.	Integrate the example and a concise version of explanatory text. Use concise audio rather than text to explain the example.
Terminology defined elsewhere (e.g., glossary)	Need to hold definition in memory to interpret the content.	Pre-teach terminology (See Tactic 16). Integrate definitions and content (for example, rollover definitions).

Figure 4.5. shows an example of one way of integrating the image from Figure 4.4 *with* the explanatory text. Figure 4.6 shows the use of a rollover to explain terminology.

MANAGE MEMORY FOR DEEPER LEARNING • 57

Figure 4.5 Integrated image and explanatory text

		Spherical	Cylinder	Axis	Add	Prism
OD: Right eye →	OD	-4.75	+2.25	090	+2.00	
OS: Left eye →	OS	-4.00	+2.25	090	+2.25	

Spherical: Lens power to correct myopia (nearsightedness)
Cylinder: Lens power to correct astigmatism
Axis: The orientation of astigmatism, in degrees
Add: Added lens power for reading

Marcus Phillips   O.D.   License: 149861

Figure 4.6 Use of rollover to explain terminology

Reply
Reply all
Forward

Reply All: Replies to *every* email address from the original message.

Charts that don't integrate text and data also require split attention. The top image in Figure 4.7 shows a chart with a legend that isn't integrated. I show how to fix this problem in the bottom image. It integrates all the information in the legend within the chart and the axes.

Figure 4.7 Diagram with split attention (top) and a solution (bottom)

Changes to temperature over time

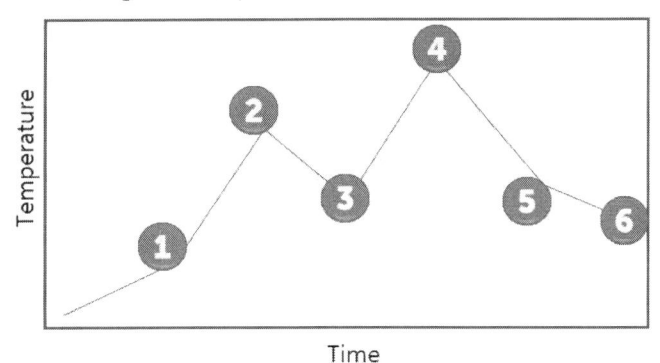

1: 1 hr, 50 degrees F
2: 2 hrs, 81 degrees F
3: 3 hrs, 69 degrees F
4: 4 hrs, 95 degrees F
5: 5 hrs, 68 degrees F
6: 6 hrs, 59 degrees F

Temperatures at every hour

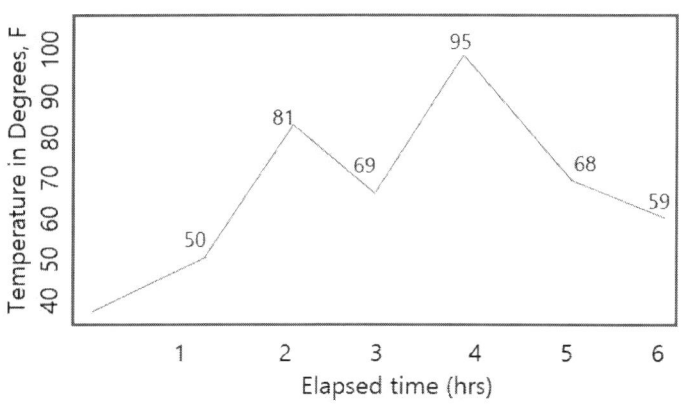

Split attention is a bigger problem for people with less prior knowledge and for more complex materials. Here are the primary ways research tells us we can avoid split attention.

- Pre-train people on background information (facts, concepts) to make content easier to understand (Tactic 16).
- Embed concise explanations when possible rather than have them separated from what they explain.
- Use a caption for a concise explanation of self-explanatory images. Leave out explanations of self-explanatory images for people with more prior knowledge.
- Present concise explanations in audio concurrently with what they explain (next section in this tactic).
- Don't ask people to process redundant information together or in close succession (following section in this tactic).

Use Audio for Explanations

One common recommendation in split attention research is using audio explanations rather than text explanations to explain still or moving images. Audio explanations reduce cognitive load by sharing processing between visual and verbal processing channels. People can *listen* to the explanation without having to move back and forth between the media and the text explanation. One nuance: The explanation needs to be simple and concise.

Using audio to explain complex visuals—like animations—can be especially helpful, according to Mayer and Moreno's well-known study about reducing cognitive load from multimedia. We find it very difficult to read explanations while also focusing on what is changing on the screen.

Avoid Redundancy

One widely misunderstood recommendation in split attention research is redundancy. People who build instruction often think that presenting *the same information* over (together or in close succession) improves learning. But research tells us otherwise. Processing redundant information together or in close succession increases mental effort.

Some examples of content that forces people to process redundant information together or in close succession:
- Presenter or instructor reading the text on their slides
- Multimedia where audio narration is the same as onscreen text
- Information largely the same as information just presented

Redundant information processed together or in close succession often creates the need to compare the sources of redundant information to see if the information is the same or different. Re-describing or re-presenting an existing and sufficient source of information should not be done. It can also cause confusion.

This advice *appears* to conflict with research telling us to offer multiple presentations of the same content (e.g., spaced learning). But we process redundant information *separated by time* separately. So, spaced learning over time helps people remember, but redundant information close together may cause confusion. I discuss spaced learning and retrieval in Tactic 19.

Don't offer redundant, simultaneous content. It causes harmful cognitive load and possible confusion.

Try It

For each of the following situations, how can you avoid split attention? My answer is on the next page, but you will learn far more by answering before reading mine!

1. Long description of how to connect your smartphone to your television along with a diagram of the connections on both devices.

2. Onscreen text describing what is happening during an animation.

3. Using a printed job aid while learning the steps to create a table of contents in Microsoft Word.

Patti's Response

1. Long description of how to connect your smartphone to your television along with a diagram of the connections on both devices.

   - Narrating the steps while showing the steps onscreen (using diagrams, animation, or video).
   - Using concise descriptions and embedding them in the diagram.

2. Onscreen text description of what is happening during an animation.

   - Narrating what is happening as the animation progresses.
   - Using concise descriptions and embedding them in the animation.

3. Using a printed job aid while creating a table of contents during a Microsoft Word training class.

   - Showing a very concise version of the job aid onscreen.

MANAGE MEMORY FOR DEEPER LEARNING • 63

Try It

For the screen shown in Figure 4.8, do you see any potential for split attention? If so, how could you avoid it? My answer is on the next page, but you will learn far more by answering before reading mine!

Figure 4.8 Split attention example

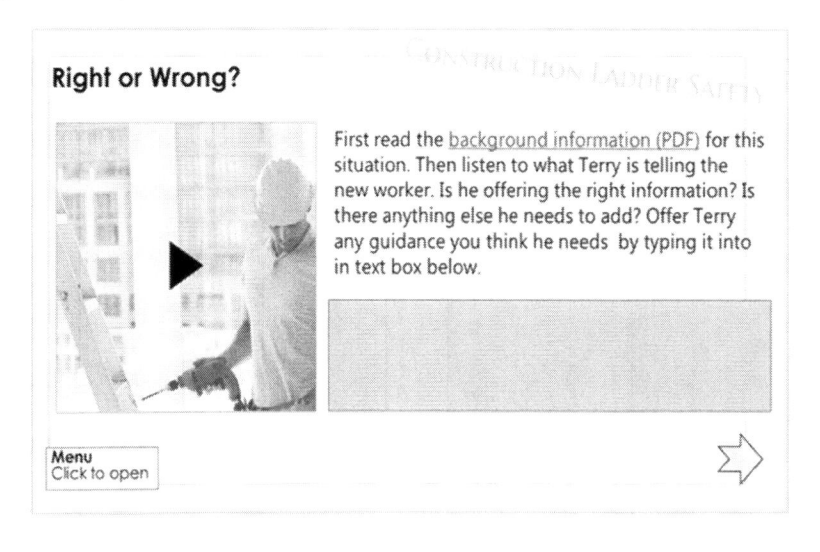

Right or Wrong?

First read the background information (PDF) for this situation. Then listen to what Terry is telling the new worker. Is he offering the right information? Is there anything else he needs to add? Offer Terry any guidance you think he needs by typing it into in text box below.

Menu
Click to open

Patti's Response

This screen calls for split attention because readers must open and read a PDF document to do the activity. They will split attention between the PDF and the video. It would be better to narrate the directions and offer the background information during the video.

Tactic 6: Allow Processing Time

Learning from instruction requires deep processing. Some instructional methods cut processing time short, however. When information is transient (quickly moving and changing), people often cannot deeply process it. For example, watching a video that shows how to replace damaged nose pads on a pair of glasses—but the video moves too fast—doesn't allow time for processing the steps. When content refers to previous information, that requires holding some content in memory to understand other content (split attention).

A video on sorting in Excel, for example, may refer to earlier content on sorting terms, such as "ascending," "descending," and "custom sort" used during formatting. If the user didn't have time to process these terms, hearing them used later in the video may decrease understanding.

Commonly used persistent and transient instructional content includes:
- *More persistent:* Text, still images, job aids, manuals
- *More transient:* Spoken text, animation, video

We know that multimedia (text, audio, still and moving images) can be beneficial for learning. Multimedia helps people "picture" what we are discussing. But, some learning is easier to process with persistent content. Research shows that multimedia may be problematic when content:
- Needs time to be deeply processed
- Is complex and needs to be studied and reviewed
- Is long

We should consider whether it makes sense to replace more persistent forms of information with transient information. For example, we might be thinking about replacing a printed or digital job aid with a video or animation. But is this a good idea? If people need to go at their own pace, review segments, or re-read earlier segments, persistent media such print or digital documents may fit the need best. In complex content or content that refers to information taught earlier, transient content can cause problems.

Guidelines for making transient information easier to process:

- Shorten segments to make them more easily reviewed
- Allow control over pace (Tactic 7)
- Use transient content when information is less complex and doesn't need to refer to earlier content
- Use with people who already understand the referenced information—or pre-train the earlier knowledge

Try It

Can you think of transient materials that would be better in a more persistent form?

Tactic 7: Offer Appropriate Control

What if we taught people to drive a car by handing them the keys and letting them try out different things to see what worked while driving? That sounds crazy, but we do something very similar in some instruction. We hand people the keys (content) and expect them to learn for themselves. Or we build a game or scenario and expect them to pick out what is critical and learn how things work on their own. Research says this is not a good practice and, too often, leads to confusion and inaccurate or incomplete understanding.

Heard the phrase, "We learn by doing?" We *can* learn by doing. But it helps if we understand what we are doing first.

The ability to make good instructional choices depends largely on prior knowledge. Without the prior knowledge to make good choices, people with less knowledge end up choosing paths that are inefficient and cause frustration. Not supplying needed guidance often results in shallow learning, gaps in understanding, and misunderstandings. I'll discuss this in much more detail in Tactic 17.

We must consider how much guidance people need to be successful. Table 4.3 describes three elements of learning control we can program into instruction or allow people to choose themselves.

Table 4.3 Control elements

Element	Description	Example
Content	Choose which objectives or segments to use.	Lana skips the first three segments as she already knows this information.
Sequence	Choose the order in which to use segments.	Marco views the segments in the Interview Techniques heading first because he begins the interviews for a graphic artist tomorrow.
Pace	Choose the speed of instruction, including starting, stopping, and continuing of the program and media elements.	Sanjay plays the videos multiple times as he is taking notes and wants to be sure he got the important information correctly written in his notes.

We know that people can and do learn on their own all the time. The question isn't *if* people can learn by making their own choices. We're asking whether *we* should guide people when we design instruction. In many cases, the answer is yes. This is especially true when people have less prior knowledge or the content is complex.

Figure 4.9 shows the interaction of prior knowledge and material complexity when deciding how much control to give to people learning.

Figure 4.9 Amount and types of learner control based on prior knowledge and complexity

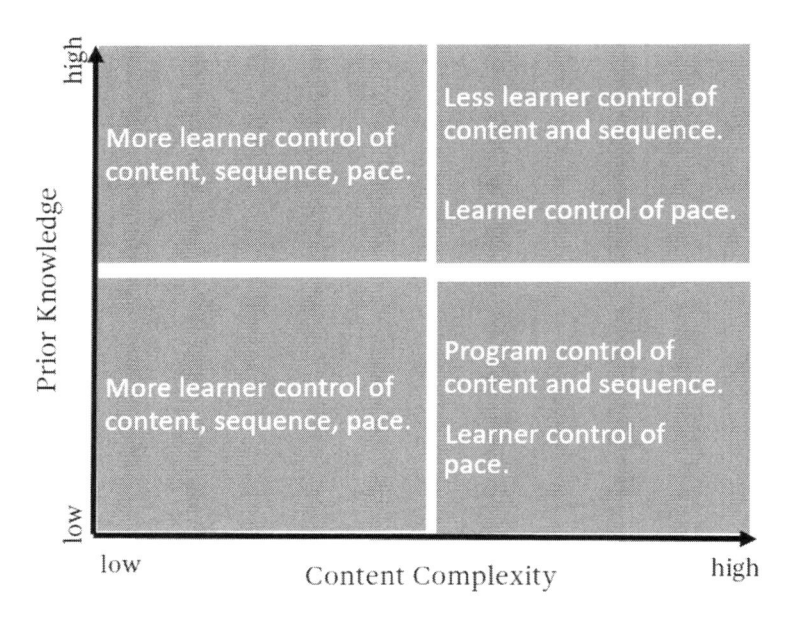

[Figure: A 2x2 matrix with Prior Knowledge (low to high) on the y-axis and Content Complexity (low to high) on the x-axis.
- High prior knowledge, low complexity: More learner control of content, sequence, pace.
- High prior knowledge, high complexity: Less learner control of content and sequence. Learner control of pace.
- Low prior knowledge, low complexity: More learner control of content, sequence, pace.
- Low prior knowledge, high complexity: Program control of content and sequence. Learner control of pace.]

When complexity is high, we should manage memory so cognitive load isn't too high. People who have less prior knowledge will learn more easily and better if we supply a best path. People with more prior knowledge may be able to control their own path, but we can offer guidance when needed.

In all these situations, allowing people to control the pace (speed) makes sense. Different people may need more or less time. They may need to start and stop and review.

Learner control of content and sequence works best for people with more prior knowledge and for less complex materials.

Deeper Practice

We have reached the end of the tactics for **Strategy 2: Eliminate Needless Mental Effort.** Select the instruction you want—or someone has asked you—to build. Then use the tactics in this chapter (recapped below) to practice eliminating needless mental effort.

Tactic 4	**Remove Unnecessary Content** Remove content that needs processing but is not valuable to the learning objectives: decorative pictures, background music, bells and whistles, and extra (unneeded) content.
Tactic 5	**Avoid Split Attention** Avoid situations that require people to hold one source of information in memory to understand another source. For example, integrate text explanations and images; or, at the very least, present them next to each other. Use audio explanations to describe still or moving images.
Tactic 6	**Allow Processing Time** When people need to review and refer to other sections (more complex content), media with more permanency makes this easier. There are ways to make more transient content (like video and animations) easier to use for this purpose.
Tactic 7	**Offer Appropriate Control** Consider prior knowledge and the complexity of the content before giving people control of content or sequence. Offering control makes the most sense when people have more prior knowledge and the materials are less complex. Allow people to control the pace whenever possible.

Consider doing this exercise with a group of people so you can discuss the following with others:
- What was helpful, less helpful?
- What did you learn?
- Which parts of this exercise will you continue to use in the future?

CHAPTER 5

Strategy 3: Make Content Easier to Comprehend

Comprehension is the ability to mentally process what we read, see, or hear. We must comprehend to understand new information, mentally integrate it with prior knowledge (in long-term memory), and use it.

Deep learning requires deep processing. Shallow processing impairs your ability to understand, remember, and apply. Reading research shows that adults often do not stop or slow down while reading to understand. They skip things that are unclear. We must make content easier for the audience to understand.

Consider being handed a prescription for a new medication. The physician says, "It's critical that you follow the directions to reduce side effects."

You get the prescription filled and the instructions say:

> Always take the dosage with water or food. Medication taken on an empty stomach is likely to produce mild to severe dyspepsia.

Does *dosage* mean *each* dose? It says to take with water *or* food. Which is better? It also says that, if taken without food (empty stomach, right?), dyspepsia is likely. What does that mean? Patient education materials, like instructional content, often has comprehension problems. And these problems negatively influence outcomes, including compliance and application.

Instructional writing is a basic skill for building content people can learn from, which is why *Write and Organize for Deeper Learning* is the first book in this series. Luckily, research has uncovered great (and actionable) insights about making written materials clear. In this chapter, I discuss content tactics that manage memory. In Tactics 8-15 (Figure 5.1), I'll discuss tactics that help people manage memory resources when using instructional content.

Figure 5.1 Tactics that manage memory resources

Tactic 8: Use Conventions
Tactic 9: Use *Their* Language
Tactic 10: Add Advance Organizers
Tactic 11: Don't Just Tell: Show
Tactic 12: Focus Attention
Tactic 13: Chunk Content
Tactic 14: Avoid Multitasking
Tactic 15: Support Memory

Tactic 8: Use Conventions

Conventions are standards established by common usage—using them improves comprehension. Many countries, for instance, have standardized signs to overcome language barriers and improve traffic safety. Sign conventions came first in Europe and, largely, other countries have adopted them.

Innovation may look and feel fun, but people do not deal well with things they don't understand. Using conventions allows people to proceed without a lot of mental effort. When we don't use conventions, people must process more new information.

Phone apps have specific conventions. For example, there are icons for certain tasks (phone and maps, for example), icons that provide status information, (for example 🔋), and icons that open apps (Facebook, Twitter, etc.). Not following conventions increases mental effort.

Use conventions to reduce mental effort.

Jakob Nielsen, the usability guru, tells us that people are unhappy when we force them to think about how to accomplish common tasks. They want websites to work like other websites. Many people use computers and the Internet all day—and having to figure out new interfaces means unnecessary work.

To show how much people want the common things they do to stay the same, Nielsen points to people *not* buying software upgrades. Part of this may be cost, but a good portion is due to the expected mental load of having to figure out what has changed and how to do familiar tasks.

Table 5.1 describes very common conventions used in information design.

Table 5.1 Information design conventions

Convention	Description	Example
Naming	Use expected names. Cute, funny, or silly names take more time to understand.	Resources vs. More!

Hierarchy	People understand and expect hierarchy (for example, book, section, chapter). Hierarchy allows people to process organization with less effort and shows content organization.	Blood Pressure
		  Diastolic
		  Systolic
		
		vs.
		
		Step 1

Navigation	Navigation should be obvious and hierarchical. Hidden navigation is widely misunderstood. Nielsen's tests on minimalist and hidden navigation showed frustration.	Blood Pressure
		  Diastolic
		  Systolic
		
		vs.
		
		•
		•
		•

Links	Typical links are blue, underlined text. Different color links are confusing. Underlined words that aren't links are confusing.	Resources vs. Resources
Buttons	Pressing an onscreen button should cause an action. Button text should clearly state what will happen. (See Naming for why naming should follow conventions.)	Submit vs. →

Try It

Review instruction you have built or are building. Are there conventions you are currently breaking that might cause unnecessary effort?

Tactic 9: Use *Their* Language

Thinking everyone will understand what you write because *you* do is like thinking your shoes will fit others because they fit you. The actual words we use make content easier to understand or harder to understand. In *Write and Organize for Deeper Learning*, I discuss the use of familiar and simple language because it is clearer. The U.S. government (as well as other governments) began campaigns to write language in "Plain Language." This means writing so others can easily read, understand, and use what we write (adapted from www.plainlanguage.gov).

Clarity

There are two tactics from *Write and Organize for Deeper Learning* that are the first steps to improving comprehension.
- Use simpler, more common words and phrases
- Use shorter sentences

These two tactics make content easier to understand. There's one more tactic we should add that makes what you write easier for your audience to understand: Use the words *they* use.

Many times, we need to teach terminology to people before we can discuss the topic. That's not what I'm talking about. Terminology is a foundation for learning a topic area and I'll discuss this in more detail in this tactic. What I'm referring to are the bulk of the words we use when writing. Figure 5.2 shows official and simpler wording used in victim's assistance program training materials.

Figure 5.2 Official versus common wording

"Official" Wording	Simple Wording
The rules in this section govern monetary and non-monetary assistance offered to victims of violent crimes, including rape, assault, battery, and homicide (and some others), and their families, for eligible expenses.	This section describes help offered to eligible violent crime victims. • Who is covered • What is covered
1 very long (31 words) and unclear sentence	1 shorter sentence (10 words), two links to cover details

Briefly, we should use the words our readers use because they don't have to think about what these words mean. In other words, they reduce the effort of understanding.

Commonly Used Words

How do we know which words are effortless for our audience and which are likely to be difficult? Tactic 1 (Analyze Prior Knowledge) and Tactic 2 (Analyze Work Tasks) will tell us a lot about what people know and the words they use. We can also analyze workers' *actual* words. The following resource makes this easy!

Resource

We can use text analysis tools to analyze the words people use. For example, you could use Word Counter and input text that workers use in documentation, emails, and collaboration tools to get a list of frequently used words and phrases. Figure 5.3 shows an analysis of the words used in the introduction to this book. I pasted in the text and Word Counter did the analysis. Voila! You're a data analyst!

Figure 5.3 Words and phrases used most often; used with permission (https://www.databasic.io/en/wordcounter)

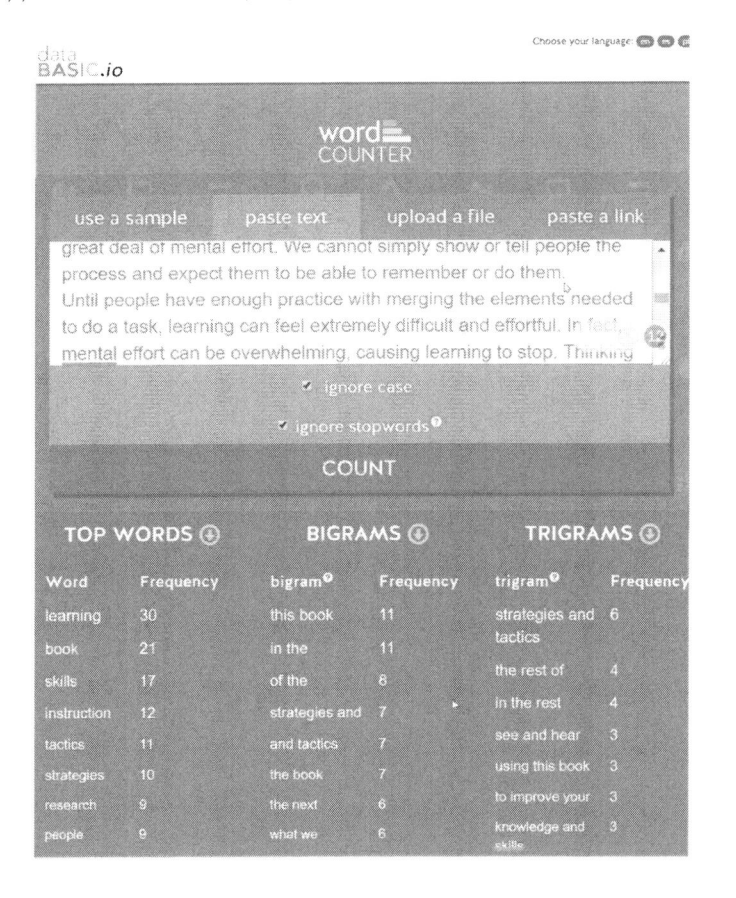

Bigrams are two-word phrases and trigrams are three-word phrases. Cool, huh?

Testing

One of the tasks usability analysts perform is user testing to see how users understand what we build. We communicate a lot through language, so it's natural we'd want to test what our words mean to users. A common user testing step is to see how users understand your interface and the words on the page. We'll concentrate on the words for this tactic. Here are two important tasks usability testers do to analyze understanding.

- Have users read the text aloud. Note where users:
    o Trip over words and phrases
    o Mispronounce words
    o Look confused
    o Ask questions
- Ask readers to summarize what they just read.

This kind of testing doesn't have to be in person. I've used webinar or screen sharing tools for this purpose.

Tactic 10: Add Advance Organizers

Near the beginning of the book, I supplied an overview of all the strategies and tactics in the book (Figure 5.4). This tactic explains the importance of introducing instruction so people understand its relevance and how it is organized.

Figure 5.4 Strategies and tactics for managing memory, from Chapter 2

	Strategy	Tactics
Chapter 3	**Strategy 1: Understand the Work**	Tactic 1: Analyze Prior Knowledge Tactic 2: Analyze Work Tasks Tactic 3: Evaluate What Must Be Remembered
Chapter 4	**Strategy 2: Eliminate Needless Mental Effort**	Tactic 4: Remove Unnecessary Content Tactic 5: Avoid Split Attention Tactic 6: Allow Processing Time Tactic 7: Offer Appropriate Control
Chapter 5	**Strategy 3: Make Content Easier to Comprehend**	Tactic 8: Use Conventions Tactic 9: Use *Their* Language Tactic 10: Add Advance Organizers Tactic 11: Don't Just Tell: Show Tactic 12: Focus Attention Tactic 13: Chunk Content Tactic 14: Avoid Multitasking Tactic 15: Support Memory
Chapter 6	**Strategy 4: Build Deep Understanding (Schemas)**	Tactic 16: Supply Missing Knowledge Tactic 17: Prefer Direct Instruction Tactic 18: Check and Fix Understanding Tactic 19: Promote Remembering Tactic 20: Build Worked Examples Tactic 21: Adapt for Prior Knowledge

Learning science discusses the value of introducing instruction with an **advance organizer.** Advance organizers may contain various types of introductory information (Table 5.2) to introduce the topic, show how topics and subtopics are related, and help people relate what they are learning to what they already know. Research shows that advance organizers help people learn and retain what they learn because they:

- Help people understand the importance of the topic and sub-topics,
- Show the structure of the content, and
- Visualize where the topic and subtopics fit into prior knowledge, which,
- Helps them organize the new information more accurately.

In this tactic, we're going to discuss the need to show the structure of the content, so people can easily understand where they are going and more accurately encode information that needs to be remembered. How we encode to-be-remembered information affects how we remember. Table 5.2 shows elements an advance organizer may include.

Table 5.2 Elements potentially included in an advance organizer

Elements	Discussion
1. Importance of the topic	Introductions—showing the broad relevance of the topic to audience needs—help people connect learning to their work.
2. Learning objectives	Well-written learning objectives help people understand the goals for instruction and how to measure their accomplishment.
3. List of topics	Listing the topics, in a hierarchy (order), helps people see the underlying structure.
4. Headings and sub-headings	Like the list of topics, the headings and sub-headings of instructional content show the framework for the instruction. Headings, sub-headings, and the list of topics should be the same.

84 • PATTI SHANK, PhD

Advance organizers may include topic and sub-topics, offering a high-level overview of how the instruction is organized. For example, the expandable menu for a medication errors course shown in Figure 5.5 lists the hierarchy of topics. The location-specific issues slide in Figure 5.6 shows that the menu item and heading are identical, reinforcing organization.

Figure 5.5 Expanding menu with list of topics

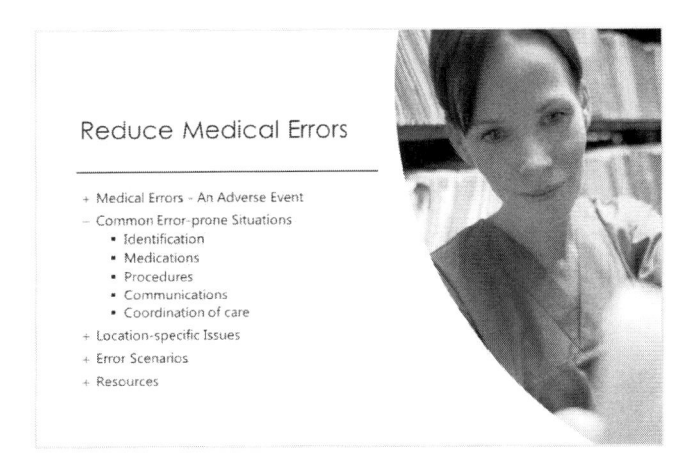

Figure 5.6 Consistent topic name in the Location-specific Issues section

Typically, we offer advance organizers *before* instruction. In print and online materials, it is often a good idea to make the advance organizer easily available. Persistent menus in online courses serve this purpose when they use user-friendly, clear language, and topic headings are the same as in the menu. Headings and sub-headings that exactly match the topics in the advance organizer lessen confusion and reinforce organization.

Tactic 11: Don't Just Tell: Show

We often supply information in visual formats because visuals *can* make information easier to understand. They fall into roughly three categories (Table 5.3).

Table 5.3 Three categories of visual representations

more realistic ↕ more symbolic	**Pictures**	Two-dimensional representations of three-dimensional reality. Still or moving images.
	Diagrams	Simplification of reality to show appearance, mechanisms, or structure. Used to reduce complexity and show hidden relationships, which are otherwise difficult to perceive. Animations can be somewhere between pictures and diagrams, depending on their realism. Newer three-dimensional representations of reality are coming (e.g., augmented reality).
	Charts	Compact presentations of mathematical data, such as bar and line graphs. They let us more easily see categories, relationships, and time passage.

In this tactic I'll discuss diagrams because they typically simplify reality. Simplification helps people focus on what is most important without the load of having to focus on everything at once. Too much visual realism can add non-relevant AND unnecessary cognitive load. Simplification is especially helpful for those with less prior knowledge.

Diagrams offer a simplified view of reality. Simplification can make less obvious relationships more obvious.

If we train homeowners on fire safety, for example, we might use diagrams like the ones shown in Figure 5.7 and 5.8.

Figure 5.7 Firepit safety elements (visual)

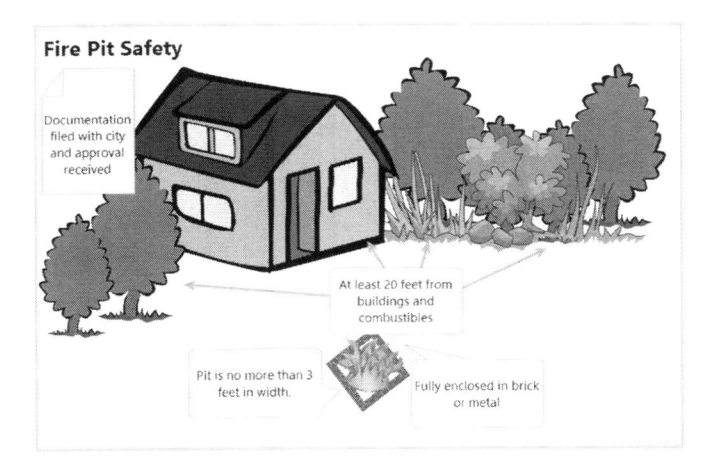

Figure 5.8 Firepit safety elements (text)

Try It

For the Figure 5.7 diagram, is the use of the images likely to add cognitive load? My answer is on the next page, but you will learn far more by answering before reading mine!

> **Patti's Response**
>
> Simplified images in this diagram point out distances between the firepit and common outdoor elements. It doesn't appear to have unneeded elements.

When is a diagram valuable?

Research shows that diagrams help learning when they:
- Are relevant
- Make important relationships visual
- Are clear to readers
- Promote deep versus surface learning
- Concisely integrate needed text
- Don't include unnecessary information

Irrelevant and unnecessary information adds unnecessary load and makes it harder to pick out important information and see relationships. The next two items (relationships, clarity) are in the eye of the beholder—so it's a good idea to test them.

A very common diagram used to help people use public transportation, for example, is a subway map. But these maps are often complex and difficult to understand. The last time I was in London I ended up going the wrong way multiple times on the Underground despite consulting subway maps.

My situation on the London Underground especially calls to mind how prior knowledge helps us interpret new information. When I lived in Washington, D.C., I had little trouble interpreting the subway map as I recognized the stops and other location information. I could mentally map the subway map to my schema of the layout of the D.C. area. This shows how accurate and usable schemas help us use information.

Make diagrams easier to understand

Research tells us to take certain steps to make diagrams easier to understand.

Table 5.4 How to make diagrams easier to understand (adapted from Davenport, Yaron, Klahr, and Koedinger)

1.	Consider prior knowledge	Create more simplified diagrams when people have less prior knowledge.
2.	Limit diagram elements to the specific learning objective	Provide only what people need.
3.	Design to make most critical understandings clear	Design specifically to highlight critical understandings. Guide attention through use of grouping, arrows, bold, etc.
4.	Make sure people correctly interpret the diagram	Build deep rather than surface learning with activities that process the diagram.

When text and diagrams provide the same information, it typically takes more effort to understand text than diagrams. But text allows us to offer nuances and ambiguities that diagrams have a more difficult time showing.

Try It

For contamination safety training, what diagram would best visualize the following concept? My answer is on the next page, but you will learn far more by answering before reading mine!

> **Control Zone Areas**
>
> Control zone areas look like a bulls-eye, with the hot zone in the center—ending at the hot line. The next zone outward is the contamination control zone, which ends at the contamination control line. The next zone outward is the cold zone, where the incident commander directs decontamination activities.

Patti's Response

Below is a diagram that visualizes the text in the exercise. How does it differ from your diagram?

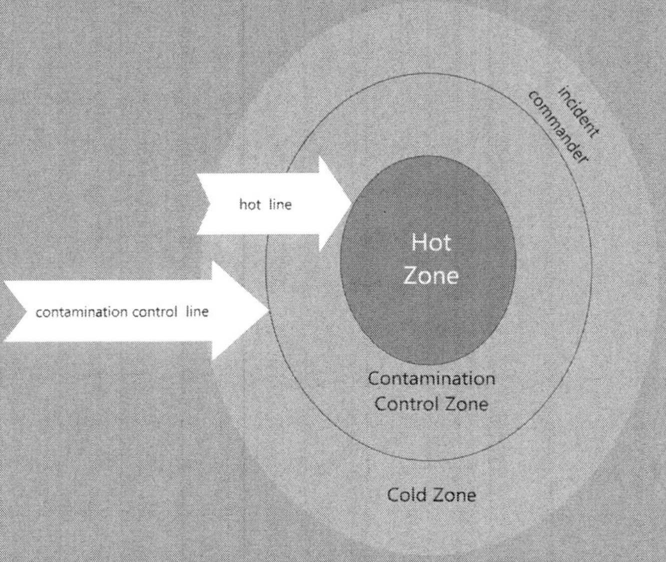
incident commander
hot line
Hot Zone
contamination control line
Contamination Control Zone
Cold Zone

Bonus points:

What could we do to make sure people come to the *right* conclusions from the diagram? Please answer before continuing. My answer is on the next page, but you will learn far more by answering before reading mine!

Patti's Response

We could ask questions that help us understand if people came to right conclusions (per the learning objectives), discuss situations, or add an activity that does the same. For example, we could ask some questions such as:
- In which zone do you think are active decontamination activities?
- In which zone is the incident commander? Why do you think she is there?

To frame questions so they are not simply "recall" activities, ask people to *interpret* the diagram. This helps people understand what the diagram means.

Resource

In this tactic, we discussed simplifying reality to make the big picture or relationships between elements clearer. How much reality should we embed in our training? Is more better? How much realism to add is outside the scope of the book, but it is an important topic. If you want to know more about what research says about realism, see my *eLearning Industry* articles on this topic:

- Realistic Training: How Realistic Should Training Be? (Part 1) https://elearningindustry.com/realistic-training-should-be-part-1
- Realistic Training: How Realistic Should Training Be? (Part 2) https://elearningindustry.com/realistic-training-realistic-training-part-2

Tactic 12: Focus Attention

Multimedia means a combination of text, audio, or still or moving images. Richard Mayer, Professor of Psychology at the University of California, has done a lot of research on what makes media easier to learn from. He explains that, when we learn from media, we must first be able to focus on what is most important. People who have less prior knowledge have a more difficult time selecting what is important.

We can help people learn from multimedia when we help people focus on what is most important.

In Tactic 4, we discussed removing materials that cause unnecessary mental effort—such as nice-to-knows and irrelevant images (such as clip art). That's a first step. We can then add *signals* to guide attention to the most critical elements.

Signals are text or image elements that emphasize specific information and help people find what is important. Sascha Schneider, Professor of Psychology at Technische Universität Chemnitz, describes two signal categories: text and pictures. Table 5.5 shows the two signal categories and common types of signals found in each category. Figures 5.9 and 5.10 show examples of text and picture signals.

Table 5.5 Signal categories and types

Signal Category	Types
Text	Heading
	Color
	Reference to images
	Combination
Pictures	Pointing
	Color
	Label
	Spotlight
	Gray out
	Combination

Figure 5.9 Headings as text signals

Tactic 13: Chunk Content

headings organizes large blocks of content into smaller, meaningful segments. The purpose for chunking is to support attention, overcome working memory limitations, and reduce the potential for overload.

Research shows that effective chunking helps people more easily process content, gain and regain attention, and reduce information overload. Attention span for large units of content is likely to wander. People who design instruction must avoid overloading memory and making it hard to focus.

Chunking helps people more easily process content and focus.

What's in a Chunk?

A chunk is a logical segment that may include text, media, and activities that belong together. To show you what I mean by "logical segment," consider a color lesson. Here's one logical way to chunk this lesson.

1. How We See Color
2. Two Color Systems
3. Primary Colors
4. Secondary Colors
5. Tertiary Colors

MANAGE MEMORY FOR DEEPER LEARNING • 97

Figure 5.10 Pointing and spotlight as picture signals

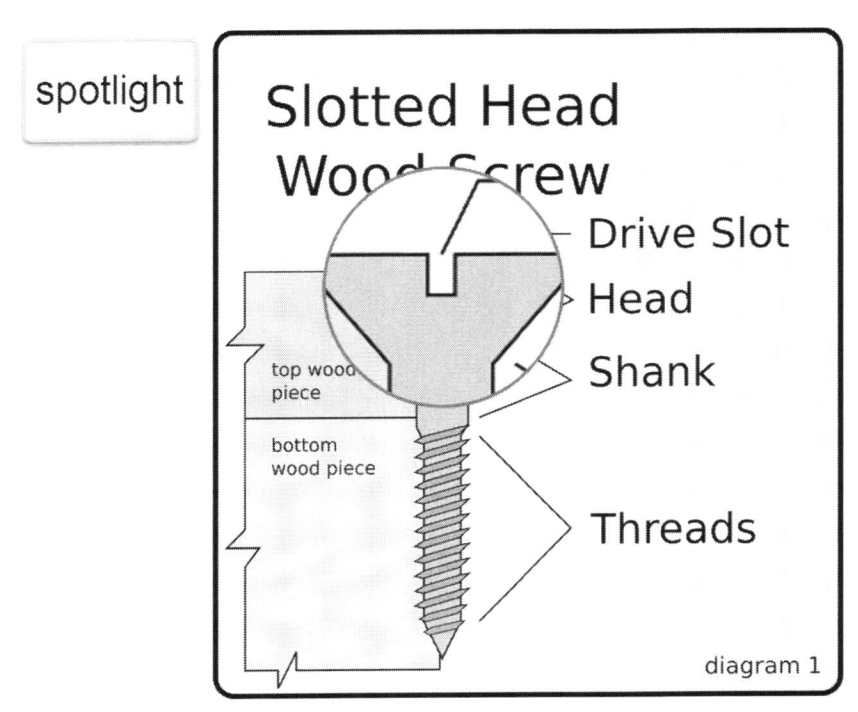

Usability research tells us not to use color as the *only* way to draw attention to specific elements, as people with color blindness may not see these signals.

In Tactic 5, I discussed the value of integrating concise explanations and labels within images. The spotlight example in Figure 5.10 shows labels integrated into the diagram rather than as a legend outside of the diagram.

Tactic 13: Chunk Content

Chunking organizes large blocks of content into smaller, meaningful segments. The purpose for chunking is to support attention, overcome working memory limitations, and reduce the potential for overload.

Research shows that effective chunking helps people more easily process content, gain and regain attention, and reduce information overload. Attention span for large units of content is likely to wander. People who design instruction must avoid overloading memory and making it hard to focus.

Chunking helps people more easily process content and focus.

What's in a Chunk?

A chunk is a logical segment that may include text, media, and activities that belong together. To show you what I mean by "logical segment," consider a color lesson. Here's one logical way to chunk this lesson.

1. How We See Color
2. Two Color Systems
3. Primary Colors
4. Secondary Colors
5. Tertiary Colors
6. Color Wheel

Figure 5.11 shows an example of the written materials for the color lesson and the first two chunks (How We See Color, Two Color Systems) and part of the third (Primary Colors). Notice the headings for each chunk match the topics and are hierarchical.

Figure 5.11 Chunks from the color lesson

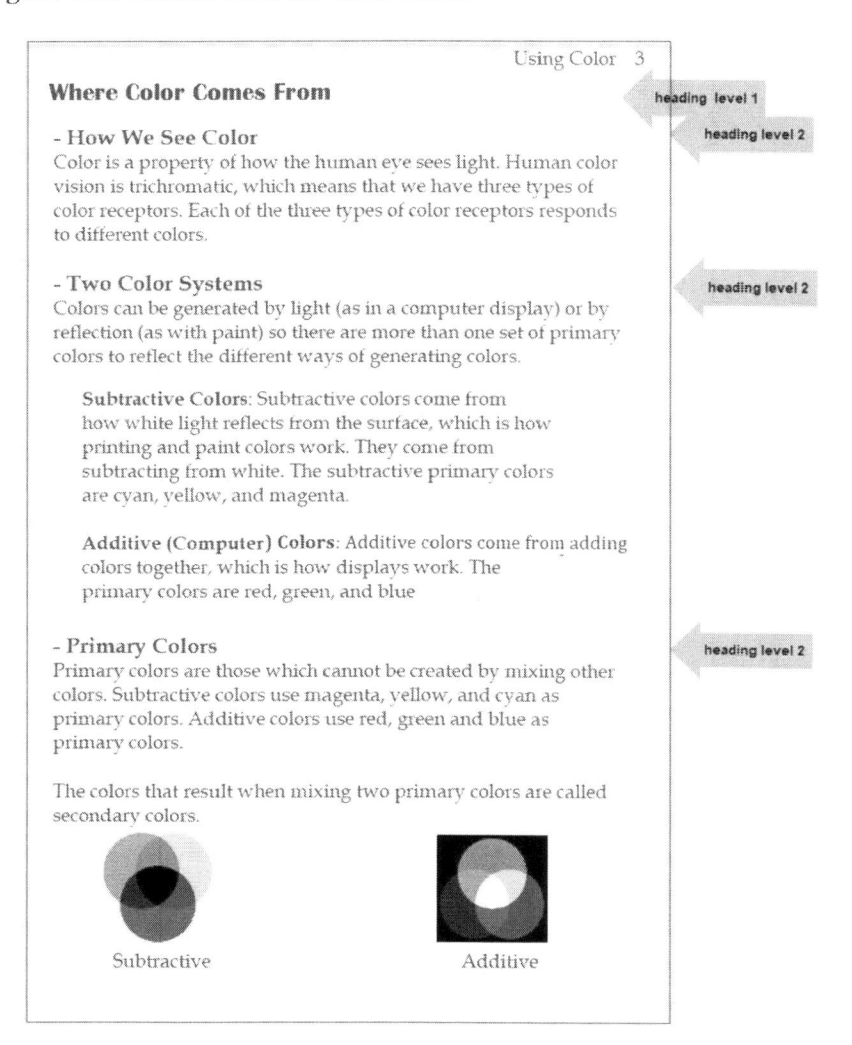

> Using Color 3
>
> **Where Color Comes From** ← heading level 1
>
> **- How We See Color** ← heading level 2
> Color is a property of how the human eye sees light. Human color vision is trichromatic, which means that we have three types of color receptors. Each of the three types of color receptors responds to different colors.
>
> **- Two Color Systems** ← heading level 2
> Colors can be generated by light (as in a computer display) or by reflection (as with paint) so there are more than one set of primary colors to reflect the different ways of generating colors.
>
> > **Subtractive Colors**: Subtractive colors come from how white light reflects from the surface, which is how printing and paint colors work. They come from subtracting from white. The subtractive primary colors are cyan, yellow, and magenta.
> >
> > **Additive (Computer) Colors**: Additive colors come from adding colors together, which is how displays work. The primary colors are red, green, and blue
>
> **- Primary Colors** ← heading level 2
> Primary colors are those which cannot be created by mixing other colors. Subtractive colors use magenta, yellow, and cyan as primary colors. Additive colors use red, green and blue as primary colors.
>
> The colors that result when mixing two primary colors are called secondary colors.
>
> Subtractive   Additive

Information delivered in right-sized chunks is easier to process and encode than unchunked content.

Chunked Versus Unchunked

Below is an example of a list of unorganized topics for a digital security module on the left and the same topics chunked on the right.

Figure 5.12 Unchunked (left) versus chunked (right) topics for digital security module (based on topics in https://myshadow.org)

- Who collects your information?
- How do they use your data?
- Location tracking
- Browser tracking
- Internet traces
- Network traces
- Hardware and software traces
- Devices
- Secure connections
- Location
- Profiles
- Email
- Surfing history
- Passwords
- Settings
- Block tracking

1. Why being safe is important
   1.1. Who collects your information?
   1.2. How do they use your data?
2. Tracking
   2.1. Location tracking
   2.2. Browser tracking
3. Traces
   3.1. Internet traces
   3.2. Network traces
   3.3. Hardware and software traces
4. Protect yourself
   4.1. Devices
   4.2. Secure connections
   4.3. Location
   4.4. Profiles
   4.5. Email
   4.6. Surfing history
   4.7. Passwords
   4.8. Settings
   4.9. Block tracking

Try It

What is different about the unchunked versus the chunked content in Figure 5.12? What can you see that makes the chunked content better for learning? My answer is below, but you will learn far more by answering before reading mine!

Patti's Response

In the unchunked topic list, topic organization isn't clear. Some of the topics are unclear without organization. When organizing the topics into chunks and giving them headings and sub-headings, we see the organization of topics and how they relate to each other.

How to Chunk Content

This section shows the typical steps for chunking content—followed by an example of the steps.

Chunking Steps

1. Create a list of needed chunks for each learning objective.
2. Categorize the chunks and give each category a name.
3. Make sure each chunk is completely relevant to the learning objective. Remove non-relevant chunks.
4. Organize and logically sequence headings and chunks. Revise names if needed.
5. If any of the chunks are too large, consider splitting.

We may need to verify chunks and organization with multiple people who understand the content. Although they may not all organize it the same way, this can help you find chunks that:

- Need to be included but aren't
- Are included but aren't needed (based on audience needs and learning objectives)
- Should ideally be placed elsewhere (sequencing problems)

Extended Example

The following example shows the chunking steps for this learning objective:

Learning objective: Build a table of contents (TOC) in a Microsoft Word document from heading styles

List of chunks for this learning objective.
How a TOC Works
TOCs and Documents
Why Use a TOC?
Types of TOCs
What Are Heading Styles?
Using Heading Styles
Build a Headings Hierarchy Using Styles
Run the TOC
Look for Problems
Redo Until Correct
Update the TOC

Categorize chunks and give each category a name.
About the TOC
    How a TOC works
    TOCs and documents
    Why use a TOC?
    Types of TOCs
Heading Styles
    What are heading styles?
    Using heading styles
    Build a headings hierarchy
      using styles

MANAGE MEMORY FOR DEEPER LEARNING • 105

Run the TOC
Look for problems
Redo until correct
Update the TOC

Make sure chunks are completely relevant and remove unnecessary chunks.

About the TOC
 How a TOC works
 ~~TOCs and documents~~
 ~~Why use a TOC?~~
 ~~Types of TOCs~~

Heading Styles
 What are heading styles?
 Using heading styles
 Build a headings hierarchy using styles
 Run the TOC
 Look for problems
 Redo until correct
 Update the TOC

Organize and logically sequence headings and chunks. Revise names if needed.

1. ~~About the TOC~~ How a TOC Works
2. ~~Headings~~ Build Headings Using Styles
    a. What are heading styles?
    b. Using heading styles
    c. Build headings hierarchy using styles
    d. Run the TOC
    e. ~~Look for problems~~ Check for and fix problems
    f. ~~Redo until correct~~ Redo running and reviewing until problems are fixed

    g.   Update the TOC

If any of the chunks are too large, consider splitting
1. How a TOC Works
2. Build Headings Using Styles
    - 2.1. What are heading styles?
    - 2.2. Using heading styles
    - 2.3. Build a headings hierarchy using styles
3. Troubleshoot the TOC
    - 3.1. Run the TOC
    - 3.2. Check for and fix problems
    - 3.3. Redo running and reviewing until problems are fixed
    - 3.4. Update the TOC

Try It

Take unchunked or poorly chunked content and chunk it.
1. Create a list of needed chunks for each learning objective.
2. Categorize the chunks and give each category a name.
3. Make sure each chunk is completely relevant to the learning objective. Remove non-relevant chunks.
4. Organize and logically sequence headings and chunks. Revise names if needed.
5. If any of the chunks are too large, consider splitting.

Tactic 14: Avoid Multitasking

Attention and focus are critical to learning, but a common practice in modern life—and in training programs—makes it more difficult to attend and focus: multitasking. Multitasking, or doing more than one task at a time, adds mental "switching costs" that reduce focus and productivity (in both tasks) and increases errors.

Researchers show that people who perform more than one task at a time do not actually multitask; they task switch. Task switching means rapidly switching between two or more tasks. Want to experience the time costs of task switching for yourself? Do each of these three tasks and time each task to the second:

Task 1: Count from 1 to 100 by tens (10, 20...)   Time=_____

Task 2: Out loud, list six words that start with the letter b.   Time=_____

Add the time for Task 1 and Task 2 together.   Total Time=_____

Task 3: Switch between the two tasks. In other words, say 10, then list a word that starts with b, then say 20, then list a word that starts with b and so forth until you have all the numbers and six words.   Time=_____

Almost everyone who does this finds that it takes longer to do Task 3 than the combined time for Task 1 + Task 2. The extra time is the switching cost of multitasking.

Trying to multitask adds "switching costs," resulting in *more*, not *less* time.

Our minds use mental control processes that help us switch tasks *without conscious awareness*. Fast switching adds mental effort and time. During the switchover, we have periods of unawareness.

The book *A Deadly Wandering* describes the story of how science came to understand the "unawareness" costs of texting and driving. People think they can easily task switch between watching the road and reading texts. They cannot.

While switching between texting and the road, the driver has lost focus on what is happening on the road and around them. As with air traffic controllers and pilots, unawareness time while task switching can have disastrous results. But, even without disastrous results, the time cost of task switching makes it problematic.

The implications for learning are clear: Do one thing at a time. When learning, focus on learning. We may be able to wash dishes while talking on the phone (both are largely automated), but we cannot learn while answering texts or emails.

For instruction:
- Help people understand the inability to focus and attend while multitasking
- Ask people to put away their phones, tablets, and laptops (unless using them for learning) during instruction
- Keep instruction lively and relevant to job tasks so people more easily pay attention

When people want to take notes during instruction, suggest using pen and paper—research shows people more easily recall written notes than typed notes. If people want to type them up later, that will provide a chance to space learning (Tactic 19) and make their notes easier to remember.

I'm not a fan of making adults do X or Y because "we say so." In my own experience asking people to not multitask; to put phones, tablets, and laptops away; and to take calls outside if they must, most people get it and comply. We cannot force people to learn, however. Adults are most motivated to learn when they see the reason, realize the content is relevant to their needs, and make up their own mind to engage.

Try It

Under what circumstances are people likely to multitask in the instruction you build? How can you gently redirect their attention and focus so doing this is less likely to occur?

Tactic 15: Support Memory

Training has limitations, including the difficulty of remembering complex skills in a short period of time. Specific tactics improve this problem: adequate practice, spaced learning, and retrieval practice. Memory support (also known as performance support) is helpful in this situation. Memory support typically takes the form of job aids and checklists (for less complex tasks) and wizards, templates, and context-sensitive help (for more complex tasks).

For example, when adding a patient to the system, an application may tell the worker what to enter in a specific field. One type of commonly used help is a rollover that describes what information to type into the field, as shown in Figure 5.13.

Figure 5.13 Rollover that shows what to enter in the field

Q Code

Q Code identifies the location. Use the primary location if more than one.

Some applications go further and tell you what to do and how to do it. An example of this kind of application is tax preparation software, which helps you with each step of the process.

When teaching people how to check in glasses, verify accuracy, and look for flaws, for example, a new optician may use a checklist during training to practice (so to not forget any the steps) and use the same checklist on the job until the steps

112 • PATTI SHANK, PhD

are automated. Training helps opticians understand the check-in process and how to apply it. But, because training is often too short for adequate practice, the same memory aid can support performance back on the job. Figure 5.14 shows an example of memory support used for checking in new glasses.

Figure 5.14 Checklist for check-in procedure

Check	√	Problems

Prescription
  OD
  OS
	☐
	☐	

PD
  Distance
  Near
	
	☐
	☐	

Multifocal type	☐	
Multifocal placement	☐	
Lens material	☐	
Lens defects	☐	
Right frame	☐	
Frame defects	☐	
Other	☐	
Clean	☐	

Figure 5.15 offers an example of more complex memory support. This support is often on the back of monthly bank statements to help people reconcile their accounts.

Figure 5.15 Memory support for reconciling your bank account

RECONCILIATION

Balancing your account means finding differences between bank records and your account records for the month. Before balancing, make sure you have:
- Your bank statement
- Your account register
- A pencil or pen
- A calculator

Step 1: Compare your bank statement and your check register

1. Compare deposits, payments, withdrawals, bank charges, and check transactions and amounts from the bank statement to your check register.
2. Add any deposits and additions that appear in your register but are not on your bank statement.

Date	Amount
Total to add:	

3. Add any checks or withdrawals that appear in your register but are not on your bank statement.

Date	Amount
Total to subtract:	

4. Add the total additions to the ending balance on your bank statement.

Total to add (from 2)	_____
Bank statement ending balance	+ _____
Subtotal	= _____

5. Subtract the total to subtract (from 3) to the subtotal in 4.

Total to subtract (from 3)	- _____
Balance	= _____

The primary reason for building memory support is because of limitations on working memory and incomplete schemas to support performance when someone has less knowledge. Table 5.6 discusses common reasons for developing and using memory support.

Table 5.6 Reasons for using memory support

Issue	*Discussion*
Tasks are complex	When learning, memory supports remembering the steps and how-tos.
Training is limited	Training time is often limited, but extended practice is needed to improve skills and remembering. Used regularly, memory support helps people perform on the job and remember.
Training outcomes are critical	When there are potentially severe negative consequences for lower performance, memory support can help people perform as needed.
Infrequent tasks	When people perform a task infrequently, remembering often suffers. Memory support can prompt the right performance.
Changing knowledge	Information or tasks that change are a signal to update prior knowledge. Memory support can prompt the changes needed and support performance while making those changes.
Training is overkill	Some tasks are small or simple and we can teach them using memory support.

Some tasks require quick action and people must know what to do without memory support—or memory support may be unlikely to be available. An example is starting CPR. When quick action is needed, memory support may be useful in training, but we must train tasks for quick remembering and automatic performance.

Try It

For instruction you are designing:
- What memory support would support memory during the course?
- Which tasks does the course teach that would benefit from memory support on the job?

Deeper Practice

We have reached the end of the tactics for **Strategy 3: Make Content Easier to Understand.** Select the instruction you want—or someone has asked you—to build. Then use the tactics in this chapter (recapped below) to practice making the content easier to understand.

Tactic 8	Use Conventions Use conventions wherever possible as they reduce the load of figuring out what to do.
Tactic 9	Use *Their* Language Use simple and clear language. Analyze the words your audience uses. Intentionally teach required new words as needed to understand the content. Test whether the audience understands what you've written.
Tactic 10	Add Advance Organizers Supply an organized overview of your content so your audience knows where you're going and how to accurately mix new information with prior knowledge.
Tactic 11	Don't Just Tell: Show Use diagrams to simplify reality and show relationships. Make sure diagrams are valuable and easy to learn from.
Tactic 12	Focus Attention Use text and picture signals to help people see what is most important.
Tactic 13	Chunk Content Chunk content into smaller, logical segments to support attention and reduce the likeliness of information overload.
Tactic 14	Avoid Multitasking Create instruction that minimizes the likelihood of task switching. Task switching reduces focus, adds time, and increases mistakes.

Tactic 15	Support Memory
	Provide tools such as job aids and checklists to help people perform while learning, remember after learning, and support performance when there is no need to remember.

Consider doing this exercise with a group of people so you can discuss the following with others:
- What was helpful, less helpful?
- What did you learn?
- Which parts of this exercise will you continue to use in the future?

CHAPTER 6

Strategy 4: Build Deep Understanding (Schemas)

This strategy is about one of the most critical outcomes of instruction: helping people build accurate and usable schemas. An optician has schemas for lenses and frames, for example—allowing her to analyze specific aspects of a person's situation (prescription, usage) and recommend specific types of frames and lenses for their needs. Her schemas come from building and modifying prior knowledge over time.

Schemas allow us to:
- Figure out what is most important
- Interpret a situation or problem
- Analyze what else we need to know
- More easily understand new information
- Solve problems

Instruction for deep learning is about building and modifying schemas.

In this chapter, we'll discuss six critical tactics that help build accurate and usable schemas.

Figure 6.1 Tactics that help people build schemas
>   Tactic 16: Supply Missing Knowledge
>   Tactic 17: Prefer Direct Instruction
>   Tactic 18: Check and Fix Understanding
>   Tactic 19: Promote Remembering
>   Tactic 20: Build Worked Examples
>   Tactic 21: Adapt for Prior Knowledge

Tactic 16: Supply Missing Knowledge

Prior knowledge is the most important factor influencing how and what we learn. How do people gain much-needed prior knowledge? Some people think experience on the job will add to prior knowledge over time.

Research shows this is not usually the case, however. K. Anders Ericsson, Professor of Psychology at Florida State University, is widely recognized as an expert in human expertise and performance. Ericsson says we should not confuse what he calls difficult and specific kinds of practice to intentionally increase expertise with normal work tasks. He tells us we typically do not improve our level of expertise through normal work tasks because we typically do work the way we already know how to do it.

The type of practice Ericsson says *does* improve expertise involves planned, goal-centered, rigorous, and often difficult practice. Today's work environments need higher levels of expertise—with its associated accurate and usable prior knowledge.

MANAGE MEMORY FOR DEEPER LEARNING • 121

Research shows that we grow prior knowledge from less complex to more complex. Figure 6.2 shows increasing levels that build on each other to build schemas and ability to apply.

Figure 6.2 Levels of knowledge (adapted from Hailikari, T., Katajavuori, N., & Lindblom-Ylanne, S.)

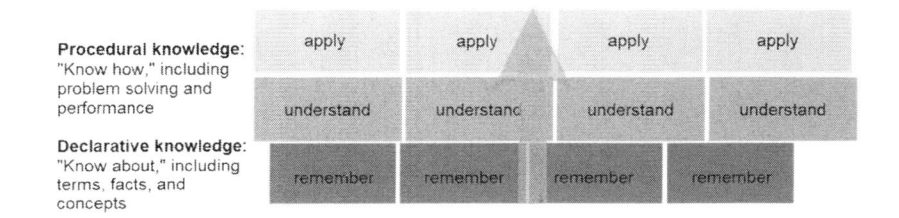

Procedural knowledge: "Know how," including problem solving and performance

Declarative knowledge: "Know about," including terms, facts, and concepts

We build on what we already know.

Table 6.1 shows examples of three levels of knowledge that medical coders—who translate medical diagnoses, procedures, services, and equipment into specific alphanumeric codes—need to learn.

Table 6.1 Levels of knowledge examples for medical coding

Level	Examples of Knowledge Needed
Remember	• Medical terminology • How each code system works • Medical records
Understand	• What does this code indicate? • Is this code correct or incorrect?
Apply	• Code the diagnoses, procedures, services, and equipment • Fix coding problems

The three levels I just described correspond to declarative and procedural knowledge. Declarative knowledge is knowledge of terms, facts, and concepts, such as when a pharmacy technician knows where the pharmacy stocks specific medications in the pharmacy. Procedural knowledge is the ability to apply, such as when the pharmacy technician verifies medications that she needs to add to stock.

Research shows that declarative knowledge is necessary for—but not enough for—application. We create a path to building usable knowledge (knowledge for application) by:

1. Analyzing **prior knowledge** to figure out what level of knowledge people already have and what they need.
2. Building **learning objectives** that clearly and specifically communicate work tasks and performance expectations.
3. Repairing **missing knowledge** and **misunderstandings.**
4. Using **research-driven tactics** to provide the right level and types of instruction to people with different amounts of prior knowledge.

Table 6.2 shows tactics for each level and commonly used activities at each level.

Table 6.2 Design for higher levels of knowledge (adapted from Hailikari, T., Katajavuori, N., & Lindblom-Ylanne, S., 2008)

Level	Tactics	Common Activities
Remember	Practice remembering (Tactic 19)	Flashcards, restate in own words, recall questions, fill-in-the-blank questions, simple games
	Space learning (Tactic 19)	Multiple and varied (types and context) presentations and practice sessions over time
Understand	Principles, implications, and interpretations (Tactic 20)	Worked examples, why and how questions, cases
Apply	Application (practice) with feedback (see *Practice and Feedback for Deeper Learning*)	Practice activities, problems, simulations, scenarios, guided on-the-job practice

We know that sequential instruction is especially important for people with less prior knowledge of the topic. Research on teaching people with lower and higher knowledge of spreadsheets showed that learning to use the application helped people *subsequently* learn how to use the application for a specified purpose. Those with prior spreadsheet knowledge, however, could deal with a non-sequential approach.

Sequencing instruction from simple to complex is most important for complex tasks and when people have low prior knowledge of the included tasks. One example is testing your blood sugar. The task includes multiple sub-steps, including preparation, getting blood, and analyzing results.

People with more prior knowledge of the included tasks may not need sequencing. This corresponds with what we know about learner control (Tactic 7). People experienced in testing their blood sugar, for example, would not need the entire sequenced instruction to use new testing equipment. They can learn any differences from what they already know.

Sequence instruction from simple to complex for people who have low prior knowledge of the included tasks.

Try It

For instruction you are designing, what do people need to remember? Understand? Apply?

Remember

Understand

Apply

Tactic 17: Prefer Direct Instruction

Workplace learning practitioners often push for "exciting" instructional methods based on inquiry and experiential (indirect) approaches. These approaches include games, scenarios, simulations, case studies, and role playing. They often mock direct instruction approaches, which directly provide knowledge and use tactics to help people remember, understand, and apply.

But hundreds of research studies show that direct rather than indirect training methods have more favorable outcomes for people with less prior knowledge.

For people with less prior knowledge, direct instruction offers better outcomes than less direct methods.

If you learned how to drive in high-school driving classes like I did, you may remember that driving training uses a sequential, direct process like Figure 6.3.

Inexperienced drivers learn at the remember level in a classroom. Driving simulations (simulator) often follows, which offers opportunities to understand and begin to apply in a safe environment. Last, people use integrated and usable knowledge in real cars on real roads. This sequential and direct process lets inexperienced drivers add complexity over time.

Figure 6.3 Simple to complex process of driving training

	Classroom	
Remember		Safety
		Vehicle control
		Traffic
		Signs, signals, and markings
		Weather
		Collisions
		Malfunctions
		Driving distracted or impaired
		Car parts
		Car maintenance
Understand	Simulator	Neighborhood driving
		Urban driving
		Highway driving
		Distractions
		Impairment
	Real Driving	Parking lot driving
		Quiet streets driving
		Busy streets driving
		Highway driving
Apply		Special circumstances
		Maintenance

Some people mistakenly equate direct instruction with rote memorization. The goal of rote memorization (e.g., state capitals, categorization of rocks) is remembering to remember. Remembering to apply is different. For example, we memorize multiplication tables not only as a math exercise, but to apply them to everyday math problems such as doubling the ingredients in a recipe.

Inquiry and experiential methods often don't specifically build needed knowledge blocks—and often increase cognitive load. We've discussed problems with missing or mistaken

knowledge. Direct instruction, on the other hand, allows people to:
- Develop knowledge from simple to complex, sequentially;
- Integrate knowledge sequentially; and
- Build needed knowledge for application.

Less direct and more experiential methods can be quite effective as practice (apply). But less direct and more experiential methods are less effective for creating the sequential building blocks of knowledge. It is less effective, more frustrating, and possibly dangerous to push people directly into practice activities without building underlying knowledge. That's like throwing children into the deep end of a swimming pool to let them "learn" how to swim without helping them learn the steps first.

There are underlying principles for direct instruction (adapted from Archer & Hughes, 2011).
1. Focus content on critical knowledge and skills.
2. Sequence skills logically (prerequisite content first, less complex to more complex, often used to less used).
3. Chunk longer content into shorter chunks, especially for those with less prior knowledge.
4. Make content organization clear.
5. Supply clear and relevant goals.
6. Use clear and concise language.
7. Activate relevant prior knowledge to assist with understanding and meaning making.
8. Help participants organize and integrate new information with prior knowledge.
9. Monitor understanding and fix as needed.
10. Model skills.

11. Guide practice closely when people have less prior knowledge.
12. Provide distributed (over time) practice.
13. Provide cumulative practice that includes previously and newly learned information.
14. Offer corrective and clarifying feedback.

You should recognize many of these principles from the strategies and tactics in this book and in *Write and Organize for Deeper Learning* and *Practice and Feedback for Deeper Learning*.

Try It

How would you apply direct instruction to instruction you are currently developing?

Tactic 18: Check and Fix Understanding

We must check understanding as people are building knowledge—because missing and inaccurate knowledge damages further learning and application. Hundreds of research studies show the learning benefits of formative assessment, which involves checking for missing and inaccurate understanding regularly. Formative assessment is not assessment for "grading" but to fix problems. Table 6.3 shows checking-for-understanding themes and shows an example of each.

Table 6.3 Methods for checking understanding

Clarity	What is least clear to you?
Comparison	Compare the two methods.
Different	How are they different?
Explain	Put this in your own words.
Implications	When should this be done?
Importance	What is the most important idea?
Same	How are they alike?
Sort	Which category does this fall under?

For example, in driver education, we could check understanding of distracted driving by discussing:
- [Same] How is distracted driving like driving while impaired?
- [Different] How are distracted driving and driving while impaired different?
- [Implications] When are we distracted? Are we aware of distractions as they occur?
- [Sort] Which of these activities are risky and which are

not?
- [Importance] Which idea is most important?

Leaving out this step is like leaving out the brackets, pegs, or pins that hold up shelving. Shelving without support doesn't support shelves—much less books. Likewise, missing information and misinformation doesn't support application.

With adults, I like to check understanding in a way that isn't embarrassing. Some virtual classroom tools, for example, allow you to create activities with anonymous responses. Figure 6.4 shows examples of anonymous poll questions used to check understanding. We could do a similar exercise with polling applications in face-to-face instruction.

Figure 6.4 Anonymous poll questions to check understanding

What is the primary purpose of formative evaluation?	How are formative and summative assessment alike? Check the best answer.
- Assess knowledge. - Gauge understanding and fix it. - See what people already know so it doesn't need to be discussed. - To see how well people understand the content. - Find out what is unclear. - What is clear and what isn't. - Whether we can move on.	☐ They assess how well participants have met learning objectives. ☐ They occur after instruction is completed. ☐ They offer data we can use to make instruction better.

After checking understanding, you will want to provide missing or inaccurate knowledge immediately and then check understanding again. The purpose of instruction is not to deliver content but build understanding and ability to apply. Try to pinpoint the source of the problem so you can fix the cause, not just the symptom.

Try It

How would you check for understanding in instruction you are currently developing? Based on your answers, how would you fix understanding?

Tactic 19: Promote Remembering

Mental effort for performing a skill is greatest when learning it—and lessens with (correct) application. Tactic 3 showed a remembering continuum and I am showing it again in Figure 6.5 to remind you of our discussion about what people must remember.

Figure 6.5 Remembering continuum

Look up ← Remember → Automate

Remembering is the ability to recall from memory. Automating means remembering *without effort*. Knowledge not used regularly typically declines. Automated skills in the workplace include many simple to complex skills that become so familiar that people might say, "I can do that in my sleep."

For example, a nurse in a hospital does not have to mentally think through the steps of taking a blood pressure reading. Nor does she have to think through (or look up) commonly used medication terminology or how to reconcile medications given with the patient's medical records. These tasks are routine and may be automated.

What Should Be Remembered? How Well?

Tactics 1 through 3 help us understand what and how well people need to remember. Can people look things up? (If yes, what do they need to remember in order to know *what* to look up, *how* to look it up, and how to *interpret* what they find?) Can people take time to think through what is needed (remember)? Or must they perform at once (automate)?

Adequate Practice

Practice is performing a behavior or task to improve outcomes or to remember (more or less automatically) what to do. But, even when reaching the desired level of performance with practice, performance will decay over time without regular use. This is exactly why we use regular practice to remember rarely used knowledge and tasks. A friend's work calls this practice "pro time," which stands for "proficiency time." Exactly.

People need far more practice time than we usually provide in training sessions. Therefore, we need to expand our notion of training to include both formal training and time outside of formal training where additional learning and practice occurs.

Practicing for improving outcomes or to remember requires more time than typical training allows. We must extend training to more than formal training events.

Spaced Learning

Spaced learning refers to multiple presentations of the same topic with a time delay between them. Research shows that learning the same content again over time helps people remember more than learning the same content in close succession (massed learning). Spacing also resists forgetting because of more and deeper processing time.

We cannot effectively process the same content again in massed learning because of redundancy issues (see Tactic 5). But we *can* effectively process the same content again when spacing learning without redundancy effects.

In case you are thinking this requires more work and time—well, you're right. But, as I've said numerous times, fast isn't enough. *It also has to work.* To free up needed time for spacing,

- Focus learning objectives on *exactly* what people need to do,
- Get rid of unnecessary content (Tactic 4),
- Help leaders and participants understand how spacing meets the organization's needs, and
- Space content inside and outside of typical training events.

Some research shows we should expand the spacings (time between repetitions of content) over time. Keeping earlier spacings closer together helps people successfully remember. Lengthen subsequent spacings so remembering requires more effort—which facilitates deeper processing. Wider spacings have shown to be better than narrower spacings—to a point. A good final spacing length will be about the same time interval that people will need to remember.

How to Space

Repeated content need not be exact repetitions of the content. To help people learn different contexts and different ways of seeing the same content, you may use content presented in different ways (for instance, video, scenarios, stories, activities, and examples). We can also use different contexts and situations. Training on caring for indoor plants, as an example, might use winter, spring, summer, and fall. Training on selecting frames and lenses might use safety, weight, size, and multifocal and single vision.

New customer service reps often get training over four to eight (or more) weeks. By week 5, however, what happens to what they learned in week 1? When information is not regularly used and recalled, it is easily forgotten. Table 6.4 shows an example of spacing content for customer service reps to reduce forgetting.

Table 6.4 Example of spacing built into customer service training

Week	Topic
1	Terminology
2	Topic A Review of earlier important topics
3	Topic B Review of earlier important topics
4	Topic C Review of earlier important topics
5	Topic D Review of earlier important topics
6	Topic E Review of earlier important topics
7	Topic F Review of earlier important topics
8	Topic G Review of earlier important topics

Retrieval Practice

Spaced learning typically involves presenting the same content again over time. It typically uses different presentation methods and contexts.

Retrieval practice has people *recall* previously learned knowledge over increasing periods of time to make it easier to retrieve over longer periods of time. Quizzes, questions, activities, and practice over time make later retrieval easier. Table 6.5 adds retrieval practice to the spaced learning shown in Table 6.4.

Table 6.5 Example of spacing and *retrieval* built into customer service training

Week	Topic
1	Terminology
2	Topic A Review of earlier important topics
3	Topic B Review of *and quiz* on earlier important topics
4	Topic C Review of earlier important topics
5	Topic D Review of *and quiz* on earlier important topics
6	Topic E Review of earlier important topics
7	Topic F Review of *and quiz* on earlier important topics
8	Topic G Review of earlier important topics
15	*Quiz on all topics*
26	*Quiz on all topics*

📎 Resource

If you want more information about spacing and retrieval practice, I recommend Will Thalheimer's report, *Spacing Learning Over Time*. It's free and available on Will's website: https://www.worklearning.com/wp-content/uploads/2017/10/Spacing_Learning_Over_Time_March2009v1_.pdf

Try It

Build a spacing and retrieval practice schedule for content you are building.

Week	Topic

Tactic 20: Build Worked Examples

When people are learning to handle complex problems, cognitive load can be very high. Worked examples help manage cognitive load in this situation.

Worked examples typically include the following parts:
- The problem
- The solution steps, in order
- The final solution

Worked examples manage cognitive load because they help people focus on critical aspects of the solution steps and the solution. You've likely seen worked examples in high school and college math.

Worked examples and how-to job aids have similarities but they have different purposes. Job aids often show the steps to complete a task. They support memory during performance (How do you do [task]? What does [acronym] mean?) Worked examples, though, have a deeper purpose. They show how to work through a situation or problem to apply it to similar problems. In the next section, I'll show a worked example on creating a worked example.

A Worked Example for Writing Worked Examples

Problem: Show people how to work through a complex problem.

> Step 1: Define the problem.

Start with a clear and specific problem statement you will show how to solve. Example:

Dialog doesn't sound realistic. (Worked example: How to write realistic dialog)

> Step 2: Decide if a worked example is the right tool.

Ask yourself whether people need to *process* the steps (worked example) or need a list of the steps (job aid)?

To write a worked example, clearly describe and show the steps. If you don't have the knowledge, you need to find a fully proficient performer who will "think aloud" or show you the steps while you document it.

MANAGE MEMORY FOR DEEPER LEARNING • 141

> **Step 3: Document the steps.**

Write out each step and add images or media as necessary. Use a less-is-more approach—include only what people need to understand the solution. Adding extra and nice-to-know content makes important information harder to pick out.

> **Step 4: Make sure the steps align with how someone who is fully proficient successfully tackles this problem or issue.**

I used "fully proficient" rather than "expert" for the same reasons as in Tactic 2. We want to offer steps that someone with less prior knowledge will be able to follow. Experts often do things differently because they know and can do more.

> **Step 5: Create activities that help participants process the worked example.**

To make sure people process worked examples, we need to add processing activities. Table 6.6 shows a progression of exercises—from assuring understanding, to being able to complete *part* of the problem, to being able to apply the example to a related problem. These activities increase in difficulty.

Table 6.6 Increasingly difficult levels of processing for a worked example

Activity	What to Do	Example
1. **Check for understanding**	Assure that people reach the correct understanding.	Which discounting method applies?
2. **Completion exercises**	Have participants complete parts of the example to show they understand it.	Calculate the discount using method 2.
3. **Application of worked example**	Use the worked example to solve a related problem.	Analyze and calculate discounts for the following situations.

Tactic 21: Adapt for Prior Knowledge

Throughout the book, I've primarily discussed tactics that are most applicable to people with less prior knowledge because of their limited working memory and limited schemas. A few tactics apply to people with more prior knowledge.

This tactic recaps the major tactics that apply to people with less prior knowledge and those that apply to people with more prior knowledge.

For people with less prior knowledge

Build content that supports memory so people with less prior knowledge *can* learn.
- Eliminate extra and just-in-case content.
- Make sure people have adequate background knowledge for what they are about to learn.
- Make sure writing is simple and clear. Test to make sure people understand what they need to understand.
- Prefer simple and concise wording.
- Use simpler diagrams.
- Focus attention using signals.
- Chunk content into smaller, coherent chunks.
- Use the same headings and sub-headings in a menu or advance organizer as the headings and sub-headings of content pages.
- Pre-train terminology and concepts if needed to understand the content.
- Explain images with narration.
- Help participants avoid multitasking.
- Use worked examples with activities to process them.

Work up to problems and application over time.
- Avoid redundant information together or in close succession.
- Check for understanding and fix any missing knowledge or misunderstandings.
- When content is complex, prefer more persistent content over transient content.
- Help people remember and apply content beyond formal training.
- Sequence content to guide and direct learning.
- Allow people control over the pace of content.
- Provide memory support during training and after.

For people with more prior knowledge

Make sure content meets their complex needs. Don't create content that gets in their way.
- Don't supply explanations for self-explanatory images.
- Keep needed explanations concise and based on prior knowledge.
- Provide opportunities for application, problem solving, exploration, and choice.

Deeper Practice

We have reached the end of the tactics for **Strategy 4: Build Deep Understanding.** Select the instruction you want—or someone has asked you—to build. Then use the tactics in this chapter (recapped below) to practice building for deeper understanding.

Tactic 16	**Supply Missing Knowledge** Make sure people have the background knowledge needed to understand and apply the instruction.
Tactic 17	**Prefer Direct Instruction** Direct rather than indirect (inquiry and experiential) training methods are preferable for people who are new to a topic. They allow people to develop knowledge from simple to complex and build needed knowledge for application. Direct instruction manages cognitive load and is more efficient and less frustrating. Less direct methods are useful once people have the needed background knowledge.
Tactic 18	**Check and Fix Understanding** We need to check for missing and inaccurate understanding regularly because these problems make it hard to continue learning and may result in inaccurate schemas.
Tactic 19	**Promote Remembering** Many tasks require remembered knowledge even when this isn't obvious. Even looking information up requires remembered knowledge of what to look up and what found information means. Three optimal ways to help people remember are practice, spaced learning, and retrieval practice.

Tactic 20	**Build Worked Examples**
	Worked examples show how to best solve specific problems. They include the problem, the solution steps, and the solution. They manage cognitive load by focusing on critical aspects of the solution steps and the solution.
Tactic 21	**Adapt for Prior Knowledge**
	Many of the tactics in this book apply *primarily* to people with minimal or nonexistent prior knowledge. These tactics help people with less prior knowledge learn despite limited working memory and limited schemas. This tactic is a recap of prior knowledge tactics from the book.

CHAPTER 7

Now What?

This chapter contains three tools to help you use the strategies and tactics in this book.

1. A **remembering practice activity** to help you remember the strategies and tactics in this book. It will be easier for you to use the tactics if you don't have to continually refer to the book.
2. A **checklist** (job aid) that lists all the strategies and tactics in the book—and a few notes to help you remember them. It's hard (but not impossible, especially if you use the retrieval practice activity) to remember 26 tactics, but the checklist will help you. Feel free to annotate them with your own notes and insights from the book.
3. A list of **references**—the research articles and books that support the strategies and tactics. I don't expect you to read them, but I want you to have them in case you want to read them.

I'd be grateful if you could tell me what you think of this book. Was the book valuable to you? Why or why not? Was it worth what you paid? You can reach out by emailing me at patti@pattishank.com. Use a descriptive subject line (such as: Comments on your Manage Memory book) so I am sure to find your email!

I use what you tell me to revise and fine-tune what I write—It makes my day! I'm especially grateful there are other learning geeks who want to make a real difference in their organizations and elsewhere. Yay!

I greatly appreciate reviews of my books on Amazon (internationally). Reviews help potential buyers decide whether it will meet their needs. Books with more reviews get more promotion on Amazon. As a self-published author, Amazon promotion makes a *huge* difference.

Thank YOU.

Retrieval Practice

Retrieval practice is a powerful learning activity for improving recall of specific information. Try to list the tactics without looking through the book. Check your answers against the table of contents or the checklist that follows. Then correct your answers and practice memorizing the right answers for five minutes. Try again in a few days. Keep doing this at slightly longer intervals.

Date: Strategies	Try 1 What are the tactics for each strategy?
Strategy 1: Understand the Work (Tactics 1–3)	
Strategy 2: Eliminate Needless Mental Effort (Tactics 4–7)	

Strategy 3: Make Content Easier to Comprehend (Tactics 8–15)	
Strategy 4: Build Deep Understanding (Tactics 16–21)	

How many did you get right?   /21

Date:	Try 2
Strategies	What are the tactics for each strategy?
Strategy 1: Understand the Work (Tactics 1–3)	
Strategy 2: Eliminate Needless Mental Effort (Tactics 4–7)	
Strategy 3: Make Content Easier to Comprehend (Tactics 8–15)	

Strategy 4: Build Deep Understanding (Tactics 16–21)

How many did you get right?   /21

Date:	Try 3
Strategies	What are the tactics for each strategy?
Strategy 1: Understand the Work (Tactics 1–3)	
Strategy 2: Eliminate Needless Mental Effort (Tactics 4–7)	
Strategy 3: Make Content Easier to Comprehend (Tactics 8–15)	

Strategy 4: Build Deep Understanding (Tactics 16–21)

How many did you get right?   /21

Date:	Try 4
Strategies	What are the tactics for each strategy?
Strategy 1: Understand the Work (Tactics 1–3)	
Strategy 2: Eliminate Needless Mental Effort (Tactics 4–7)	
Strategy 3: Make Content Easier to Comprehend (Tactics 8–15)	

Strategy 4: Build Deep Understanding (Tactics 16–21)

How many did you get right?   /21

Manage Memory for Deeper Learning Checklist

Use this job aid as memory support for the strategies and tactics in this book. The descriptions to the right of the tactics are concise recommendations distilled from the book.

Strategy 1: Understand the Work

Tactic 1	Analyze Prior Knowledge Figure out which direct and indirect methods you can use to find out the prior knowledge level of your audience.
Tactic 2	Analyze Work Tasks Document the tasks and sub-tasks, problems, decisions, and knowledge elements for tasks to be learned.
Tactic 3	Evaluate What Must Be Remembered Find out what people need to commit to memory and what they can look up. Where on the remembering continuum is what they need to remember?

Strategy 2: Eliminate Needless Mental Effort

Tactic 4	**Remove Unnecessary Content** Remove content that needs processing but is not valuable to the learning objectives: decorative pictures, background music, bells and whistles, and extra (unneeded) content.
Tactic 5	**Avoid Split Attention** Avoid situations that require people to hold one source of information in memory to understand another source. For example, integrate text explanations and images; or, at the very least, present them next to each other. Use audio explanations to describe still or moving images.
Tactic 6	**Allow Processing Time** When people need to review and refer to other sections (more complex content), media with more permanency makes this easier. There are ways to make more transient content (like video and animations) easier to use for this purpose.
Tactic 7	**Offer Appropriate Control** Consider prior knowledge and the complexity of the content before giving people control of content or sequence. Offering control makes the most sense when people have more prior knowledge and the materials are less complex. Allow people to control the pace whenever possible.

Strategy 3: Make Content Easier to Understand

Tactic 8	Use Conventions Use conventions wherever possible as they reduce the load of figuring out what to do.
Tactic 9	Use *Their* Language Use simple and clear language. Analyze the words your audience uses. Intentionally teach required new words as needed to understand the content. Test whether the audience understands what you've written.
Tactic 10	Add Advance Organizers Supply an organized overview of your content so your audience knows where you're going and how to accurately mix new information with prior knowledge.
Tactic 11	Don't Just Tell: Show Use diagrams to simplify reality and show relationships. Make sure diagrams are valuable and easy to learn from.
Tactic 12	Focus Attention Use text and picture signals to help people see what is most important.
Tactic 13	Chunk Content Chunk content into smaller, logical segments to support attention and reduce the likeliness of information overload.
Tactic 14	Avoid Multitasking Create instruction that minimizes the likelihood of task switching. Task switching reduces focus, adds time, and increases mistakes.
Tactic 15	Support Memory Provide tools such as job aids and checklists to help people perform while learning, remember after learning, and support performance when there is no need to remember.

Strategy 4: Build Deeper Understanding

Tactic 16	**Supply Missing Knowledge** Make sure people have the background knowledge needed to understand and apply the instruction.
Tactic 17	**Prefer Direct Instruction** Direct rather than indirect (inquiry and experiential) training methods are preferable for people who are new to a topic. They allow people to develop knowledge from simple to complex and build needed knowledge for application. Direct instruction manages cognitive load and is more efficient and less frustrating. Less direct methods are useful once people have the needed background knowledge.
Tactic 18	**Check and Fix Understanding** We need to check for missing and inaccurate understanding regularly because these problems make it hard to continue learning and may result in inaccurate schemas.
Tactic 19	**Promote Remembering** Many tasks require remembered knowledge even when this isn't obvious. Even looking information up requires remembered knowledge of what to look up and what found information means. Three optimal ways to help people remember are practice, spaced learning, and retrieval practice.
Tactic 20	**Build Worked Examples** Worked examples show how to best solve specific problems. They include the problem, the solution steps, and the solution. They manage cognitive load by focusing on critical aspects of the solution steps and the solution.

| Tactic 21 | **Adapt for Prior Knowledge**
Many of the tactics in this book apply *primarily* to people with minimal or nonexistent prior knowledge. These tactics help people with less prior knowledge learn despite limited working memory and limited schemas. This tactic is a recap of prior knowledge tactics from the book. |

Want More?

The Deeper Learning Series shows you how to apply information and usability, learning, cognition, writing psychology, and other applicable research to your instructional projects. The other books in the series include:

Write and Organize for Deeper Learning, which tackles four strategies and 28 tactics. You can find it on Amazon, internationally.
Strategy 1: Understand Your Audience's Need
Strategy 2: Write for Clarity
Strategy 3: Make Text Readable and Legible
Strategy 4: Organize for Memory and Use

Practice and Feedback for Deeper Learning, which discusses five strategies and 26 tactics. You can find it on Amazon, internationally.
Strategy 1: Analyze the Job Context
Strategy 2: Practice for Self-direction
Strategy 3: Practice for Transfer
Strategy 4: Practice for Remembering
Strategy 5: Give Effective Feedback

If you want to offer Deeper Learning books to a team, I can help you get quantity discounts.

I can train your team, group, or conference group, and supply discounted Deeper Learning series books for these sessions. Contact me at patti@pattishank.com.

My goal is to make it easier for *anyone* who writes learning content (including content experts, instructional designers, teachers, and instructors) build deeper instruction. Just. That. Simple.

What Is the Readability of This Book?

The readability score of the text in this book is 61, which is equivalent to approximately 7th grade. I use ProWritingAid (https://prowritingaid.com) to do readability testing because it also helps me find sentences that are too long, words that are overused, and clichés.

	Grade Level Measures		Other Measures	
61	Flesch-Kincaid Grade	7.1	Flesch Reading Ease	61.3
FLESCH READING EASE	Coleman-Liau	10.7	Dale-Chall	5.2
Target > 60	Automated Readability Index	7.0		
	Dale-Chall Grade	5 - 6		

Later versions of Microsoft Word (usually under Word Options) include readability statistics based on Flesch Reading Ease, which is the same readability score shown above. This readability scale uses scores from 0 to 100. The higher the number, the easier the text is to read. I wanted readability to be around 60 because I didn't want readability to be an issue for *anyone*.

References

This list includes references that support the insights and recommendations in this book. You likely will find many of these references online by searching for the authors' last names and the title of the paper. If you can't find a paper, it should be available in academic libraries.

Adult Skills, Job Skills

Levy, F. & Murnane, R. J. (2013). Dancing with robots: Human skills for computerized work. Third Way & NEXT.

OECD Skills Outlook https://www.oecd.org/skills/piaac

World Economic Forum. (January 2016). The Future of Jobs: Employment, Skills and Workforce Strategy for The Fourth Industrial Revolution. http://reports.weforum.org/future-of-jobs-2016/

Rotman, D. (June 12, 2013). How technology is destroying jobs. MIT Technology Review.

Check Understanding (Formative Assessment)

Sadler, D. Royce. (1989). Formative assessment and the design of instructional systems. Instructional Science, 18(2), 119–144.

Advance Organizers

Ausubel, D. P. (1960). The use of advance organizers in the learning and retention of meaningful verbal material. Journal of Educational Psychology, 51, 267-272.

Ausubel, D. (1978). In defense of advance organizers: A reply to the critics. Review of Educational Research, 48, 251-257.

Bruning, R. H., Schraw, G. J., Norby, M. M., & Ronning, R. R. (2003). Cognitive psychology and instruction (4th ed.). Upper Saddle River, NJ: Merrill Prentice Hall.

Locke, E. A. & Latham, G. P. (2002). Building a practically useful theory of goal setting and task motivation: A 35 year odyssey. American Psychologist, 57(9), 705-717.

Locke, E. A. & Latham, G. P. (2006). New directions in goal-setting theory. Current Directions in Psychological Science 15(5), 265-268.

Mayer, R. (2003) Learning and Instruction. New Jersey: Pearson Education, Inc.

Simon, B. & Taylor, J. (2009). What is the value of course-specific learning goals? Journal of College Science Teaching, 39, 52-57.

Cognitive Load

Bennett, S. J., Maton, K. A., & Kervin, L. K. (2008). The 'digital natives' debate: A critical review of the evidence. British Journal of Educational Technology, 39 (5), 775-786.

Brown, C. & Czeriewicz, L. (2010). Debunking the digital 'native': Beyond digital apartheid, towards digital literacy. Journal of Computer Assisted Learning, 26(5), 357-369.

Blayney P., Kalyuga S., & Sweller J. (2015) Using cognitive load theory to tailor instruction to levels of accounting students' expertise, Educational Technology and Society, 18(4), 199 – 210.

Bodie, G. D., Powers, W.G., & Fitch-Hauser, M. (2006). Chunking, priming and active learning: Toward an innovative and blended approach to teaching communication-related skills. Interactive Learning Environments, 14(2), 119-135.

Chung, J. & Davies, I.K. (1995). An instructional theory for learner control: Revisited. In: Proceedings of the 1995 Annual National Convention of the Association for Educational Communications and Technology (AECT).

Cooper, G. (1998). Research into Cognitive Load Theory and Instructional Design at UNSW
http://dwb4.unl.edu/Diss/Cooper/UNSW.htm

Dosher, B. A. & Rosedale, G. (1989). Integrated retrieval cues as a mechanism for priming in retrieval from memory. Journal of Experimental Psychology: General, 118, 191-218.

Kalyuga S., Ayres P., Chandler P., & Sweller J. (2003). The expertise reversal effect, Educational Psychologist, 38(1), 23 – 31.

Kalyuga S., Chandler, P. A., & Sweller J. (2001). Learner experience and efficiency of instructional guidance, Educational Psychology, 5 - 23

Kalyuga S., Chandler P., & Sweller J., 1998, 'Levels of expertise and instructional design,' Human Factors: the journal of the human factors and ergonomics society, 40(1), 1 – 17.

Koch, I. & Hoffmann, J. (2000). Patterns, chunks, and hierarchies in serial reaction-time tasks. Psychological Research, 63, 22-35.

Johnstone, A. H. & Percival, F. (1976). Attention breaks in lectures. Education in Chemistry, 13(2), 49-50.

Lawless, K.A. & Brown, S.W. (1997). Multimedia learning environments: Issues of learner control and navigation, Instructional Science 25, 117–131.

Leahy W. & Sweller, J. (2005). Interactions among the imagination, expertise reversal, and element interactivity effects, Journal of Experimental Psychology: Applied, 11 (4), 266 – 276.

Miller, G.A. (1956). The magical number seven, plus or minus two: Some limits on our capacity for processing information.

Psychological Review, 63, 81-97.

Mayer, R. E. (2001). Multimedia Learning. New York: Cambridge University Press.

Mayer, R. E. & Moreno, R. (2003). Nine ways to reduce cognitive load in multimedia learning. Educational Psychologist, 38(1), 43-52.

Mayer, R. E. & Anderson, R. B. (1991). Animations need narrations: An experimental test of a dual-coding hypothesis. Journal of Educational Psychology, 83, 484–490.

Mayer, R. & Chandler, P. (2001). When learning is just a click away: Does simple user interaction foster deeper understanding of multimedia messages? Journal of Educational Psychology, 93(2), 390-397.

Mayer, R. E., Heiser, J., & Lonn, S. (2001). Cognitive constraints on multimedia learning: When presenting more material results in less understanding. Journal of Educational Psychology, 93, 187–198.

Mayer, R. E. & Moreno, R. (2003). Nine ways to reduce cognitive load in multimedia learning, Educational Psychologist, 38(1), 43–52.

Murphy, M. (2007). Improving learner reaction, learning score, and knowledge retention through the chunking process in corporate training. Dissertation.

Nesbit, J.C. & Adesope, O.O. (2006). Learning with concept and knowledge maps: A meta-analysis. Review of Educational Research, 76(3), 413-448.

Nerb, J., Ritter, F. E., & Langley, P. (2007). Rules of order: Process models of human learning. In F. E. Ritter, J. Nerb, T. O'Shea, & E. Lehtinen (Eds.), In order to learn: How the sequences of topics affect learning. 57-69. Oxford University Press.

Meyer, K. (2016). How Chunking Helps Content Processing. Nielsen Norman Group. https://www.nngroup.com/articles/chunking

Paas, F. G. W. C & Van Merriënboer, J. J. G. (1993). The efficiency of instructional conditions: An approach to combine mental effort and performance measures. Human Factors: The Journal of the Human Factors and Ergonomics Society, 35(4): 737–743.

Paas, F. & Sweller, J. (2012). An evolutionary upgrade of cognitive load theory: Using the human motor system and collaboration to support the learning of complex cognitive tasks. Educational Psychology Review, 24(1), 27–45.

Pollock, E., Chandler, P., & Sweller, J. (2002). Assimilating complex information. Learning and Instruction, 12, 61-86.

Spanjers, I., van Gog, T., Wouters, P. & van Merriënboer, J. (2012). Explaining the segmentation effect in learning from animations: The role of pausing and temporal cueing. Computers & Education, 59(2), 274–280.

Stern, E. (2017). Individual differences in the learning potential of human beings.

Sweller, J. (1994). Cognitive load theory, learning difficulty and instructional design. Learning and Instruction, 4, 295-312.

Sweller, J. (2005). Implications of cognitive load theory for multimedia learning. In R. E. Mayer (Ed.), The Cambridge Handbook of Multimedia Learning (pp. 19-30). New York, NY: Cambridge University Press.

Sweller, J. (2008). Human cognitive architecture. In J. M. Spector, M. D. Merrill, J. V. Merriënboer, & M.P. Driscoll (Eds.), Handbook of Research on Educational Communications and Technology 3rd ed., 369-381. New York, NY: Taylor & Francis Group.

Sweller, J. (2010). Element interactivity and intrinsic, extraneous, and germane cognitive load. Educational Psychology Review, 22, 123-138.

Sweller, J. and Chandler, P. (1994). Why some material is difficult to learn. Cognition and Instruction, 12, 185-233.

van Merriënboer, J.G. & Sweller, J. (2005). Cognitive load theory and complex learning: Recent developments and future directions, Educational Psychology Review, 17(2).

Comprehension

Jakob Nielsen. (January 1, 2011). Top 10 Mistakes in Web Design.
Richards, S. (2017). Content Design. Nielsen Norman Group. www.nngroup.com/articles/top-10-mistakes-web-design

Sherwin, K. (July 20, 2014) Breaking Web Design Conventions = Breaking the User Experience. Nielsen Norman Group. www.nngroup.com/articles/breaking-web-conventions

U.S. Government Plain Language Program
https://www.plainlanguage.gov Note that other governments have similar programs. Search for country name and "Plain Language."

Cues

Schneider, S., Beege, M., Nebel, S., & Rey, G. D. (2018). A meta-analysis of how signaling affects learning with media. Educational Research Review, 23, 1-24.

Deep Learning

Beatie, V., Collins, B., & McInnes, B. (1997). Deep and surface learning: A simple or simplistic dichotomy? Accounting Education, 6(1), 1-12.

Bjork, R. A. (1994). Memory and metamemory considerations in the training of human beings. In J. Metcalfe and A. Shimamura (Eds.), Metacognition: Knowing about knowing. pp. 185–205.

Chin, C. & Brown, D. E. (2000). Learning in science: A comparison of deep and surface approaches. Journal of Research in Science Teaching. 37(2), 109-138.

Craik, F. I. M. & Lockhart, R. S. (1972). Levels of processing: A framework for memory research. Journal of Verbal Learning and Verbal behavior, 11, 671-684.

Craik, F.I.M. & Tulving, E. (1975). Depth of processing and the retention of words in episodic memory. Journal of Experimental Psychology: General, 104, 268-294.

Haggis, T. (2003) Constructing Images of Ourselves? A Critical Investigation into "Approaches to Learning" Research in Higher Education. British Educational Research Journal, 29, 1, 89-104.

Hall, M., Ramsay, A. & Raven, J. (2004) Changing the learning environment to promote deep learning approaches in first year accounting students. Accounting Education 13, 489-505.

Lee, H.W. Lim, K.Y., Grabowski, B.L. (2008). Generative learning: Principles and implications for making meaning. In J. M. Spector, M.D. Merrill, J. van Merriënboer, & M.P. Driscoll, (Eds.) Handbook of Research on Educational Communications and Technology (3rd ed.).

Marton, F. & Säljö, R. (1976). On qualitative differences in learning. I. Outcome and process. British Journal of Educational Psychology, 46, 4-11.

Marton, F. & Säljö, R. (1997). Approaches to learning. In F. Marton, D. J. Hounsell, & N. J. Entwistle (Eds.), The Experience of Learning (2nd ed.). Edinburgh: Scottish Academic Press.

Merrill, M. D. (2002). First principles of instruction. Educational Technology, Research and Development, 50(3), 43–59.

Merrill, M. D. (2007). First principles of instruction: A synthesis. In R. A. Reiser & J. V. Dempsey (Eds.), Trends and issues in instructional design and technology (2nd ed., pp. 62–71). Upper Saddle River, NJ: Pearson.

van Merriënboer, J. J. G. & Kirschner, P. A. (2017). Ten steps to complex learning. Routledge.

Design Science

van Aken, J. E. & Romme, G. (2012) Reinventing the future: adding design science to the repertoire of organization and management studies, Organization Management Journal, 6(1), 5-12.

Brünken (Eds.), Instructional design for multimedia learning, 181-195. Münster: Waxmann.

Narciss, S. (2012). Feedback in instructional contexts. In N. Seel (Ed.), Encyclopedia of the Learning Sciences, Volume F(6), pp. 1285-1289. New York: Springer Science & Business Media.

Nicol, D. & Macfarlane-Dick, D. (2006). Formative assessment and self-regulated learning: a model and seven principles of good feedback practice. Studies in Higher Education, 31, 199–218.

Shute, V. J. (2007). Focus on Formative Feedback Educational Testing Service, Princeton, NJ.

Diagrams

Davenport, J. L., Yaron, D., Klahr, D. & Koedinger, K. (2008). When do diagrams enhance learning? A framework for designing relevant representations. ICLS 2008 Proceedings of the 8th International Conference for the Learning Sciences, 191-198.

Larkin, J. H. & Simon, H. A. (1987). Why a diagram is (sometimes) worth ten thousand words. Cognitive Science, 11, 65-99.

Scaife, M. & Rogers, Y. (1996). External cognition: How do graphical representations work? International Journal of Human-Computer Studies, 45(2), 185-213.

Schnotz, W. (2005). An Integrated Model of Text and Picture Comprehension. The Cambridge Handbook of Multimedia Learning.

Direct Instruction

Archer, A. L. & Hughes, C.A. (2011). Explicit Instruction: Effective and Efficient Teaching. New York, NY: The Guildford Press.

Kirschner, P. A., Sweller, J., & Clark, R. E. (2006). Why minimal guidance during instruction does not work: An analysis of the failure of constructivist, discovery, problem-based, experiential, and inquiry-based learning. Educational Psychologist, 41(2), 75-86.

Stockard, J., Wood, T. W., Coughlin, C., & Khoury, C. R. (2018). The effectiveness of direct instruction curricula: A meta-analysis of a half century of research. Review of Educational Research.

Expertise

Clark, R. (2003). Building expertise: Cognitive methods for training and performance improvement (2nd ed.). Silver Spring, MD: International Society for Performance Improvement.

Ericsson, K. A., Krampe, R. Th., & Tesch-Römer, C. (1993). The role of deliberate practice in the acquisition of expert performance. Psychological Review, 100(3), 363-406.

Ericsson, K. A. (2016). Peak: Secrets from the new science of expertise. Boston: Houghton Mifflin Harcourt.

Macnamara, B. N., Hambrick, D. Z., and Oswald, F. L. (2014). Deliberate practice and performance in music, games, sports, education, and professions: a meta-analysis. Psychological Science.

Fidelity

Alexander, A. L., Brunyé, T., Sidman, J., & Weil, S. A. (2005). From gaming to training: a review of studies on fidelity, immersion, presence, and buy-in and their effects on transfer in pc-based simulations and games. DARWARS Training Impact Group.

Learnability

Costabile, M. F., De Marsico M., Lanzilotti R., Plantamura, V. L., & Roselli, T. (2005). On the usability evaluation of e-learning applications. Proceedings of the 38th Hawaii International Conference on System Sciences.

Grossman, T., Fitzmaurice, G., and Attar, R. (2009). A survey of software learnability: metrics, methodologies, and guidelines. In Proceedings of the 27th international Conference on Human Factors in Computing Systems. New York, NY, 649-658.

Guthrie, J. T. (1972). Learnability versus readability of texts. The Journal of Educational Research, 65(6).

Memory, Cognitive Architecture

Atkinson, R. C. & Shiffrin, R. M. (1968). Human memory: A proposed system and its control processes. In K. W. Spence & J. T. Spence, The Psychology of Learning and Motivation: II. Oxford, England: Academic Press.

Ausubel, D. P. (1968). Educational Psychology: A Cognitive View. New York: Holt, Rinehart & Winston.

Baddeley, A. (1992). Working memory. Science, 255, 556-559

Bennett, S. J., Maton, K. A. & Kervin, L. K. (2008). The 'digital natives' debate: A critical review of the evidence. British Journal of Educational Technology, 39 (5), 775-786.

Bjork, R.A. (1994). Memory and metamemory considerations in the training of human beings. In J. Metcalfe, J. & Shimamura, A. (Eds.), Metacognition: Knowing about Knowing, 185-205. Cambridge, MA: MIT Press.

Brown, C. & Czeriewicz, L. (2010). Debunking the digital 'native': Beyond digital apartheid, towards digital literacy. Journal of Computer Assisted Learning, 26(5), 357-369.

Chen, B. & Hirumi, A. (2009). Effects of advance organizers on learning for differentiated learners in a fully Web-based course. International Journal of Instructional Technology & Distance Learning.

Craik, F.I.M. & Lockhart, R.S. (1972). Levels of processing: A framework for memory research. Journal of Verbal Learning and

Verbal Behavior, 11, 671-684.

Gustafson, K.L. (2000). Designing technology-based performance support. 40(1), 38-44.

Rossett, A. & Schafer, L. (2007). Job Aids & Performance Support, John Wiley & Sons.

Sheu, F. (2001). Activity theory framework and cognitive perspectives in designing technology-based support systems. Annual Proceedings of the Association for Educational Communications and Technology.

Tulving, E. & Craik, F. I. M. (2000). The Oxford handbook of memory. Oxford: Oxford University Press.

Multitasking, Task Switching

Gopher, D., Armony, L., & Greenspan, Y. (2000). Switching tasks and attention policies. Journal of Experimental Psychology: General, 129, 308-229.

Monsell, S. & Driver, J., Eds. (2000). Control of cognitive processes: Attention and Performance XVIII. Cambridge, Mass.: MIT Press.

Rubinstein, J. S., Meyer, D. E. & Evans, J. E. (2001). Executive Control of Cognitive Processes in Task Switching. Journal of Experimental Psychology: Human Perception and Performance, 27, 763-797.

Performance

Rummler, G. A. & Brache A. (1995). Improving performance: How to manage the white space on the organization chart. San Francisco: Jossey-Bass.

Wallace, G. W. (2006). Modeling mastery performance and systematically deriving the enablers for performance improvement, in Pershing, J.A. (Ed.) Handbook of Human Performance Technology, Third Edition.

Prior Knowledge

Bhargava, S., Loewenstein, G., & Sydnor, J. (2017). Choose to lose: Health plan choices from a menu with dominated option, The Quarterly Journal of Economics, 132 (3), 1319–1372.

Hailikari, T., Katajavuori, N., & Lindblom-Ylanne, S. (2008.) The relevance of prior knowledge in learning and instructional design. American Journal of Pharmaceutical Education, 72 (5) Article 113.

Clarke, T., Ayres, P., & Sweller, J. (2005). The Impact of Sequencing and Prior Knowledge on Learning Mathematics through

Spreadsheet Applications. ETR&D, 53(3), –24 ISSN 1042–1629.

Dochy, F., De Rijdt, C., & Dyck, W. (2002). Cognitive prerequisites and learning. Active Learning in Higher Education, 3(3) 265–284.

Portier SJ & Wagemans JJM. The assessment of prior knowledge profiles: a support for independent learning? Distance Education. 1995, 16, 65–87.

Strangman, N., Hall, T., & Meyer, A. (2004). Background knowledge instruction and the implications for UDL implementation. Wakefield, MA: National Center on Accessing the General Curriculum.

Remembering

Cepeda, N. J., Vul, E., Rohrer, D., Wixted, J. T., & Pashler, H. (2008). Spacing effects in learning a temporal ridgeline of optimal retention. Psychological Science, 19, 1095-1102.

Dunlosky, J., Rawson, K. A., Marsh, E. J., Nathan, M. J., & Willingham, D. T. (2013). Improving students' learning with effective learning techniques: Promising directions from cognitive and educational psychology. Psychological Science in the Public Interest, 14, 4-58

Self-direction

Duckworth, A. L. & Seligman, M. E. P. (2005). Self-discipline outdoes IQ in predicting academic performance of adolescents. Psychological Science, 16, 939-944.

Duckworth, A. L., Gendler, T. S., & Gross, J. J. (2016). Situational strategies for self-control. Perspectives on Psychological Science, 11, 35-55.

Locke, E. A. & Latham, G. P. (2002). Building a practically useful theory of goal setting and task motivation. A 35-year odyssey. American Psychologist, 57(9), 705-17.

Nilson, L. B. (2013). Creating Self-Regulated Learners: Strategies to Strengthen Students' Self-Awareness and Learning Skills. Sterling, VA: Stylus Publishing.

Oettingen, G. (2014). Rethinking positive thinking: Inside the new science of motivation. New York, NY: Penguin.

Oettingen, G. & Mayer, D. (2002). The motivating function of thinking about the future: Expectations versus fantasies. Journal of Personality and Social Psychology, 83, 1198-1212.

Oettingen, G., Pak. H., & Schnetter, K. (2001). Self-regulation of goal setting: Turning free fantasies about the future into binding goals. Journal of Personality and Social Psychology, 80, 736-753.

Rana, S., Ardichvili, A., & Poesello, D. (2016). Promoting self-directed learning in a learning organization: tools and practices. European Journal of Training and Development, 40, 470-489.

Sitzmann, T. & Ely, K. (2011). A meta-analysis of self-regulated learning in work-related training and educational attainment: What we know and where we need to go. Psychological Bulletin, 137(3), 421-42.

Spacing, Retrieval Practice

Benjamin, A. S. & Tullis, J. (2010). What makes distributed practice effective? Cognitive Psychology, 61, 228-247.

Caple, C. (1997). The effects of spaced practice and spaced review on recall and retention using computer-assisted instruction. Dissertation Abstracts International: Section B: The Sciences & Engineering, 57, 6603.

Chi, M. T. H. (2000). Self-explaining expository texts: The dual processes of generating inferences and repairing mental models. In R. Glaser (Ed.), Advances in instructional psychology (pp. 161–238). Mahwah, NJ: Lawrence Erlbaum Associates, Inc.

Chi, M. T. H., Bassok, M., Lewis, M., Reimann, P., & Glaser, R. (1989). Self-explanations: How students study and use examples in learning to solve problems. Cognitive Science, 13, 145–182.

Chi, M. T. H., DeLeeuw, N., Chiu, M.-H., & LaVancher, C. (1994). Eliciting self-explanations improves understanding. Cognitive Science, 18, 439–477.

Dempster, F.N. (1990). The spacing effect: A case study in the failure to apply the results of psychological research. American Psychologist, 43, 627-634.

Dempster, F. & Farris, R. (1990). The spacing effect: Research and practice. Journal of Research and Development in Education, 23(2), 97-101.

Karpicke, J. & Blunt, J. (2011). Retrieval practice produces more learning than elaborative studying with concept mapping. Science, 331(6018). 772-775.

Lehmann-Willenbrock, N. & Kauffeld, S. (2010). Sales training: Effects of spaced practice on training transfer. Journal of European Industrial Training.

McNamara, D.S., Kintsch, E., Songer, N.B., & Kintsch, W. (1996). Are good texts always better? Interactions of text coherence, background knowledge, and levels of understanding in learning from text. Cognition and Instruction, 14(1), 1-43.

Roediger, H.L. & Karpicke, J.D. (2006). The power of testing memory: Basic research and implications for educational practice. Perspectives on Psychological Science, 1, 181-210.

Roediger, H.L. & Karpicke, J.D. (2006). Test-enhanced learning: Taking memory tests improves long-term retention. Psychological Science, 17, 249-255.

Roediger, H. L. & Butler, A. C. (2011). The critical role of retrieval practice in long-term retention. Trends in Cognitive Sciences. 15 (1): 20–27.

Split Attention

Ayres, P. & Sweller, J. (2005). The split-attention principle in multimedia learning. In (Ed) The Cambridge Handbook of Multimedia Learning, 1st Edition, 135-146.

Chandler, P., & Sweller, J. (1992). The split-attention effect as a factor in the design of instruction. British Journal of Educational Psychology. 62(2), 233–246.

Elliott, S. N., Kurz, A., Beddow, P., & Frey, J. (2009). Cognitive load theory: Instruction-based research with applications for designing tests. Proceedings of the National Association of School Psychologists.

Kalyuga, S., Chandler, P., & Sweller, J. (1999). Managing split-attention and redundancy in multimedia instruction, Applied Cognitive Psychology, 13, 351-371.

Kalyuga, S., Chandler, P., & Sweller, J. (2004). When redundant on-screen text in multimedia technical instruction can interfere with learning. Human Factors, 46(3), 567-581.

Mayer, R. & Anderson, R. (1991). Animations need narrations: An experimental test of a dual-coding hypothesis. Journal of Educational Psychology, 83, 484-490.

Mayer, R. and Anderson, R. (1992). The instructive animation: Helping students build connections between words and pictures in multimedia learning. Journal of Educational Psychology, 84, 444-452.

Task Analysis

Clark, R. E., Feldon, D., van Merriënboer, J., Yates, K., & Early, S. (2007). Cognitive task analysis. In Spector, J. M., Merrill, M. D., van Merriënboer, J. J. G., & Driscoll, M. P. (Eds.) Handbook of research on educational communications and technology (3rd ed.). Mahwah, NJ: Lawrence Erlbaum Associates.

Crandall, B. Klein, G. & Hoffman, R. R. (2006). Working Minds, A Practitioner's Guide to Cognitive Task Analysis. MIT Press.

Jonassen, D. H., Tessmer, M., & Hannum, W. H. (1999). Task Analysis Methods for Instructional Design. Lawrence Erlbaum Associates.

Training Outcomes

Salas, E., Tannenbaum, S.I., Kraiger, K., & Smith-Jentsch, K.A. (2012). The science of training and development in organizations: What matters in practice, Psychological Science in the Public Interest, 13 (2), pp. 74-101. 42.

Williams, J. & Rosenbaum, S. (2004). Learning Paths. San Francisco: Pfeiffer.

Transfer

Baldwin, T. T. & Ford, J. K. (1988). Transfer of training: A review and directions for future research. Personnel Psychology, 41, 63–105.

Burke, L.A. & Hutchins, H.M. (2007). Training transfer: An integrative literature review. Human Resource Development Review, 6, (3), 263-296.

Burke, L. and Hutchins, H. (2008). A study of best practices in training transfer and proposed model of transfer, Human Resource Development Quarterly, 19, 107–28.

Foxon, M. (1993). A process approach to the transfer of training. Australian Journal of Educational Technology, 9(2), 130-143.

Grossman, R. & Salas, E. (2011). The transfer of training: What really matters. International Journal of Training and Development, 15(2), 103-120.

Salas, E., Wilson, K. A., Priest, H. A., & Guthrie, J. W. (2006). Design, Delivery, and Evaluation of Training Systems, in Handbook of Human Factors and Ergonomics, Third Edition (ed G. Salvendy), Hoboken, NJ: John Wiley & Sons, Inc.

Worked Examples

Renkl, A. (2005). The worked-out examples principle in multimedia learning. In Mayer, R.E. (Ed.), The Cambridge Handbook of Multimedia Learning. Cambridge: Cambridge University Press.

Renkl, A. (1997). Learning from worked-out examples: A study on individual differences. Cognitive science, 21(1), 1-29.

Renkl, A., Atkinson, R. K., & Große, C. S. (2004). How fading worked solution steps works—a cognitive load perspective. Instructional Science, 32(1-2), 59-82.

Sweller, J. (2006). The worked example effect and human cognition. Learning and Instruction, 16(2) 165–169.

Workplace Changes

Brynjolfsson, E. & McAfee, A. (2012). Race against the machine: How the digital revolution is accelerating innovation, driving productivity, and irreversibly transforming employment and the economy. Lexington: Digital Frontier Press.

Brynjolfsson, E. & McAfee, A. (2016). The second machine age: Work, progress, and prosperity in a time of brilliant technologies. New York: WW Norton & Company.

Chui, M., Manyika, J., & Miremadi, M. (November 2015). Four fundamentals of workplace automation, McKinsey Quarterly.

Christensen, C. M. (1997). The Innovator's Dilemma: When New Technologies Cause Great Firms to Fail. Harvard Business Review Press.

Wastlund, E. (2007). Experimental Studies of Human-Computer Interaction: Working memory and mental workload in complex cognition.

Index

A

advance organizer 82–85
analyze work tasks 36
    content experts vs. excellent
        performers 37
attention 95

B

bigrams, trigrams 81
Bjork, Robert 25

C

check understanding 129–31
chunking 99–106
clarity 78
cognitive load 22–24
comprehension 73
conventions 74

D

declarative and procedural
    knowledge 122
deep learning 25–26
    desirable difficulties 25
    differences between surface and
        deeper learning 25
deep processing 73
diagrams 86–90
direct instruction 125–28
    underlying principles 127
dual-channel processing 19

E

encoding 16
Ericsson, K. Anders 120
expertise 120

F

familiar and simple language 78
fidelity 94
formative assessment 129
four strategies and 21 tactics 29

H

Hoffman, Robert R. 39

I

instructional writing 74

K

Kalyuga, Slava 33
Klein, Gary A. 39

L

learnability/readability 28
learner to program control 68
learning by doing 68
learning sciences............................. 2

M

Marton, Ference 25
Mayer, Richard 95
memory 9–17
    encoding 16
    long-term memory 14
    retrieval..................................... 16
    sensory memory 11
    working memory....................... 12
memory support 111–15
missing and inaccurate knowledge
  129
multitasking 108–9

N

narration 19, 59
Nielsen, Jakob 75

P

persistent and transient content ... 65
practice 133

R

prior knowledge .. 3, 143–44, 68, 121, 143–44
    analyze prior knowledge............32
    direct measures of knowledge ..33
    indirect measures of knowledge 32
processing time 65

R

readability
    readability score of this book .. 163
redundant content 60
reference list 164
remembering
    adequate practice....................133
    analyze the need for remembering
   43
    evaluate what must be remembered 39
    remember versus automate 42, 132
    remembering continuum...42, 132
    why we must remember 41
remember-understand-apply 122
Retrieval Practice..........................136

S

Säljö, Roger....................................25
schema 14–15
    build schema........................14–15
sequencing 123–24
signals.......................................95–98
spaced learning 134–35

split attention 54
Sweller, John 23, 33

T

text analysis 80

U

unnecessary content 48

user testing 81

W

Wallace, Guy 39
worked examples 139–42
Working Minds
  A Practitioner's Guide to Cognitive
  Task Analysis 39

About the Author

Patti Shank is an internationally recognized learning analyst, researcher, designer, and author who is cited as one of the leading international workplace learning experts. She works with people and organizations to find optimal research-driven solutions and is regularly asked to speak at conferences and train trainers, instructors, designers, and experts.

Patti completed her PhD from the University of Colorado, Denver, focusing on interaction and tools for interaction in learning. Her research on new online learners won an EDMEDIA best research paper award.

She has authored, co-authored, or edited many learning books and eBooks. You can find her recent articles at eLearning Industry (elearningindustry.com/members/patti-shank-phd) and on her own blog (www.pattishank.com/blog). She lives in Colorado, USA, in close view of the eastern front range of the Rocky Mountains.

Printed in Great Britain
by Amazon